"Christian has written an inspiring boc
people realize the God-given purpose fo.
in need of direction to read this book."

—Mattress Mack,
Owner of Gallery Furniture, Philanthropist

"In *Second Wind*, Christian artfully weaves personal stories, philosophy, and scripture to infuse hope and faith into each devotional. If you are looking to blaze a new trail or if you just need motivation to keep going on the path that you're already on, read this book to find inspiration."

—Dinesh and Debbie D'Souza,
Political commentators, Author, and Filmmaker

"Our true and proper purpose is worship, prayer, and meditation focused on our merciful God as Paul wrote in Romans. With a few sentences of meditation each day, Christian captures the essence of an attentive focus on worship in spending quiet and purposeful time with our loving and gracious Father. God is pleased when our worship is thoughtful. With notable quotes and key Bible verses, Christian leads us into reverent meditation in a wonderful book that guides us day-by-day and year-to-year in reflection on God our maker. *Second Wind* will always be close at hand in my home."

—Lt. Gen. Steve Hummer, US Marines (Retired)

"Rarely does someone have the opportunity to read an author's life before reading the author's book. Thankfully, I've had the privilege of personally observing Christian's extraordinary life that inspires and empowers the extraordinary words within this book. This daily devotional will help you begin every day adjusting your mindset toward thought-provoking and life-guiding truths, proven effective by the life of the author who delivers it."

—Pastor Jason Shepperd, Church Project

"*Second Wind* by Christian Collins is a wonderful devotional book designed to encourage busy people of all ages in their daily walk with the Lord. Each day includes a quote from a notable person, then a devotional word of wisdom from Christian, closing with a key scripture to meditate on. Christian's material is exceptionally original and inspirational. This is an excellent way to start or end each day!"

—Dr. Dave and Betty Anderson,
Grace Theological Seminary and Montgomery County Eagle Forum

"In this excellent daily devotional that will motivate you to stay on track with your "living," Christian addresses the subjects that we all need to live up to the call of God in a succinct but powerful way. I recommend this resource as an excellent way to start your day."

—Pastor Steve Riggle, Grace Woodlands

"Christian is an up-and-coming Christian leader who has developed a wonderful resource for believers from all walks of life to be encouraged. In just a few moments a day, this book will inspire and challenge Christ followers to draw closer to Him and dig deeper into His Word. In the incredibly hectic schedules of most people in our time, anyone can in a few brief minutes use this outstanding tool to start the day, finish it, or both, stronger in their walk of faith in Jesus Christ!"

—Reverend Dave Welch, Texas Pastors Council

"Everyone needs God every day, and *Second Wind* provides a daily devotional to stay connected to God's Word. Michelle and I find our days are better when we start and end the day with the Word of God. I look forward to adding *Second Wind* to our daily reading and encourage you to do the same. Our strength comes from God, and we are grateful for Christian's new book that speaks biblical truths into the lives of others."

—Gordy and Michelle Bunch,
Owners of The Woodlands Financial Group, Chairman of The Woodlands Township Board

"When it comes to serving people and giving back, Christian doesn't only talk the talk, he walks the walk. He was there with me at Caney Creek Cowboy Church day in and day out, serving the people of Montgomery County during Hurricane Harvey. I have so much respect and admiration for this young man and love him. In this book, you will find that God has a plan, and Christian helps you understand you're a part of that plan. I highly recommend everyone get this book and read it."

—**Pastor Mark Grimes**, Caney Creek Cowboy Church

"A 'second wind' is defined as 'a new strength or energy to continue something that is an effort.' Many times, runners will run with partners who can provide just the right amount of encouragement and challenge to help them find that new strength and energy to run the race before them, especially when it is difficult. Christian Collins is that running partner for you and me in the Christian life, which the Apostle Paul likened to a race. In *Second Wind*, Christian gives us a daily dose of verses from God's Word, inspiring quotes, insightful illustrations from real life, and personal encouragement to help us find that second wind. Each daily devotional is brief but meaningful, removing any excuse of "not enough time" to not start your day off right. This is one of those books you will want to buy several copies to give as gifts as a way to encourage others."

— **Reverend Scot Wall**,
Capitol Commission and Magnolia Bible Church

"The daily grind of life has a way of draining our souls and clouding the reason and purpose God has for our lives. Christian has given us a tool that not only lifts your spirit, but clears the fog of why you are here and what God wants to do in your life. If you are in need of a second wind, and who isn't, *Second Wind* is a breath of fresh air!"

—**Dr. James T. Gross**, West Conroe Baptist Church

"In his daily devotional, *Second Wind*, Christian Collins captures inspiration, hope, and faith through thought-provoking quotes from historical figures, both spiritual and secular. He is then able to infuse these words of wisdom with his own personal experiences and the Holy Scriptures in a way that truly feeds the spirit."

—**Pastor Gary Buckaloo**, Church of the Good Soldier

"Christian is both insightful and inspirational. This daily devotional is saturated in Scripture, making *Second Wind* not only a breath of fresh air in a spiritually polluted culture, but also an instrument of grace employed by the Holy Spirit to purify our consciousness and breathe life into our souls."

—**Reverend Jason J. Nelson**, Rose Hill United Methodist Church

"Devotional classics are somewhat antiquated, difficult, and often out-of-touch. Christian Collins has redefined the devotional with *Second Wind*, a daily guide to breaking through the chatter of a 24/7 world and entering into the peace that only God can give. Insightful, meaningful, purposeful—the messages found in this book will draw you into the abundant life Jesus has for you. You will want to buy it, read it, and share it. Most importantly, through God you will find your second wind to take the next step, climb the next mountain, and embrace the possibilities God has for you."

—**Pastor Ken Gurley**, First Church of Pearland

"Early in ministry, I learned the importance of spending time every day with God. Christian has provided an excellent tool to serve as a catalyst for busy people to pause, think, and pray about God's will for their lives before launching another day. In less than two minutes each day, Christian provides healthy nourishment for the soul using anecdotes from famous people and insight from Scripture."

—**Dr. Rick Scarborough**, Recover America Now

FOREWORD BY RAFAEL CRUZ

SECOND WIND

A 365-DAY DEVOTIONAL TO PURSUING GOD'S GREATER CALLING

CHRISTIAN COLLINS

LUCIDBOOKS

Published by Lucid Books in Houston, TX

www.LucidBooksPublishing.com

This book is dedicated to my parents,
Chet and Mimi.
I'm so grateful for your love, wise counsel, and prayers
that have kept me through the years.

FOREWORD

I met Christian Collins in April 2015 when we were starting the presidential campaign for my son, Senator Ted Cruz. Christian and I traveled all over the United States doing pastors' conferences and speaking at many churches, all scheduled and coordinated by Christian. He has the endurance of a long-distance runner, and the title of this book applies very well to his life. Not only did he participate with me in at least three meetings a day, six days a week for a year and a half, but he also drove me from place to place under constant criticism from me about his poor driving habits. Christian is a very cautious driver, which exasperated me, and I would tell him, "You have time to pass," but he would wait until the road was totally clear. But in spite of my constant badgering, not once did he respond!

On our so-called rest day, Christian would write a report of the results of the week and spend countless hours on the phone making sure our schedule for the following week was all in place.

When the presidential campaign was over, I was able to reflect on my relationship with Christian, and I suddenly realized what a great testimony of Christ-like character Christian had been all that time we were campaigning. We began spending time together in person and over the phone, primarily in prayer and sharing the riches of the Word of God. His servant-leadership began to open doors for him, and he became the campaign manager for Congressman Kevin Brady. He did an outstanding job and put together an incredible campaign team. Almost immediately, he began organizing a pastors' coalition and organizing multiple prayer breakfasts. I had the privilege to speak at most of them with Christian and Congressman Brady.

Christian's commitment to the Lord and his impeccable integrity have not been unnoticed by various candidates who are seeking his wise counsel. He is widely respected by pastors and those who are familiar with what he has accomplished. But most of all, what defines Christian are his commitment to the Lord and his desire to be at the center of His will, the primary subject of every conversation and prayer we have together. I consider Christian one of my closest friends and my prayer partner.

As I read through the pages of *Second Wind*, I see a young man in intimate communion with his Lord who is seeking a glimpse of His glory and His wisdom while trying to make sense of the ups and downs of daily life—the ups and downs that can easily distract or even derail our walk with the Lord. I am certain the reader will identify with many of the situations Christian describes in this magnificent devotional. Like him, they may find the path back to a close relationship with his or her Lord and be able to experience the abundant life that is only found in Him.

I encourage the reader to start the day with this devotional and your Bible and allow the Holy Spirit to illuminate your path so you may be able to walk in the fulness of His glory.

"Thy word is a lamp unto my feet, and a light unto my path" (Ps. 119:105 KJV).

Reverend Rafael B. Cruz
Grace for America

INTRODUCTION

The prophet Elijah was quite the long-distance runner. Scripture teaches in 1 Kings 18 that God gave him the strength to outrun King Ahab's chariot all the way to Jezreel. That was between 17 and 30 miles, and chariots pulled by strong horses ran as fast as 35–40 miles per hour. It seems improbable that any human being could run that fast, but we know that with God, all things are possible. In 1 Kings 19, Elijah ran away from Queen Jezebel because she threatened to kill him, and perhaps he ran just as fast that time. After Elijah was as far away from Jezebel as he could get, he begged God. "I have had enough, LORD," he said. "Take my life; I am no better than my ancestors" (1 Kings 19:4). Elijah would rather die than face the seemingly all-powerful Jezebel. Moreover, we can deduce that the lives of many of Elijah's ancestors probably did not fare very well. Nevertheless, Elijah's destiny was not to die in that moment but rather to finish the race that God had set before him. Eventually, God got Elijah back on the right track, but not before Elijah wasted his time and energy running in the wrong direction.

I have a feeling that where Elijah was spiritually, psychologically, and emotionally is where a lot of Christ-followers find themselves at times. I can attest that I have battled fear. One moment I feel as if I am on course and running my race with boldness and courage, and the next, I feel like I am sidetracked by worry and discouragement. Although Frederick Nietzsche was opposed to Christianity, he did make a wise point that has

1

always stuck with me. He said that life is simply "long obedience in the same direction."* Above all else, we must stay obedient to God and the leading of His Holy Spirit. Like Elijah, we can allow fear to hinder us from going where God is beckoning us. Moreover, we may even believe we are no better off than our relatives, but we cannot allow their sins and mistakes to prohibit us from moving forward. The calling on each of our lives is too great for us to allow temporary setbacks to stop us from finishing the race God has set before us.

While the title of this 365-day devotional book—*Second Wind*—has a running theme, most of the daily devotionals are not about running. I have intertwined biblical stories, personal stories, and a bit of theology and philosophy to hopefully inspire you to look to Christ to find your second wind. This book is not just for runners but for anyone struggling to move forward in the direction God is calling them after facing setbacks. Whether it's college students feeling lost finding direction for their lives, single moms overwhelmed with bills and the struggles of life, employees striving for purpose in their work, teenagers struggling with their identities in Christ, empty nesters who feel aimless trying to find what's next in their lives, business owners on the verge of bankruptcy, or starving artists feeling as if they are running out of time, we all need renewing. We all need our second wind. I pray that this book inspires you to go to God as the source of your renewed strength so you can reach your full potential and fulfill your God-given purpose in Jesus.

---

* Friedrich Nietzsche, *Beyond Good and Evil*, (South Kingstown, RI: Millennium Publications, 2014), 46.

SECOND WIND

A 365-Day Devotional to Pursuing God's Greater Calling

January 1: Finding Satisfaction

God is most glorified in us when we are most satisfied in Him.
—John Piper

What satisfies you? Perhaps it's a home-cooked meal after a long day of work or the warmth of a child or spouse who greets you after you've been away on a trip. Maybe it's a retirement account after you begin to see a return on your investments. These are all things we hope to enjoy if we aren't enjoying them already, and yet none of them would matter if we were dying of dehydration. If we were that thirsty, we would do whatever we could to find water to quench our thirst. King David said, "As the deer pants for streams of water, so my soul pants for you, my God" (Ps. 42:1). Though David knew the temporary pleasures of wealth, power, and fame—none of which were inherently bad to enjoy—they were the poorest of substitutes for the rich supremacy of a God who is eternally good. May we, too, make it our chief desire to bring God glory by finding our true satisfaction in Christ.

Satisfy us in the morning with your steadfast love, that we may rejoice and be glad all our days (Ps. 90:14 ESV).

January 2: God's Favor and Discipline

We often learn more of God under the rod that strikes us than under the staff that comforts us.
—Stephen Charnock

More than once, King David veered off the straight and narrow in his life, and God disciplined him for it. But David said, "For his anger lasts only a moment, and his favor lasts a lifetime" (Ps. 30:5). In other words, David realized it would be much worse had God left him to his vices, but it was because God favored David that He disciplined him. God chooses to discipline the people He has a purpose for. Though David was not without sin, he had a general pattern of repenting of his sin to continue being obedient to God, thus living in such a way as to bring God glory. It's no wonder God called him "a man after my own heart" (Acts 13:22). May we, too, be people who recognize the favor of God in our lives through His discipline so when He does choose to discipline us, we will immediately correct our course, repent, and have a general pattern of living obediently to Him in order to bring Him glory.

For the Lord disciplines those he loves, and he punishes each one he accepts as his child (Heb. 12:6 NLT).

January 3: **Hearing God's Voice**

If God is speaking to your heart, don't let your mind get in the way of what God wants you to do.
—Mark Batterson

Some dreams God puts in our hearts can only be born on our knees. In other words, we have to spend the necessary time in fervent prayer, asking God to move mightily on our behalf while submitting ourselves to His purpose, and that is when God begins to reveal His plans for us. If anyone doesn't know what God is calling them to do in their current season of life, then recognize that it is God's character to fill our lives with purposes that are so much greater than just living for our own desires. May we call out to God and ask Him to speak to us in ways we can undeniably recognize as His voice.

Many are the plans in a person's heart, but it is the Lord's purpose that prevails (Prov. 19:21).

January 4: Vision Requires Grit

Continuous effort—not strength nor intelligence—
is the key to unlocking our potential.
—Winston Churchill

When God gives us visions for our future, He also requires us to have the grit to see those visions to fruition. Each day, we must set and accomplish our short-term goals so we get closer to realizing our long-term visions. Talent is great to have, but grit will beat talent in the long run because grit is simply a matter of working hard and having the resolve to persist through life's adversities and live up to our potential. Empowered by the Holy Spirit, we can do just that, so let's pray today that we will supplement the visions God has given us with grit.

You need to persevere so that when you have done the will of God, you will receive what he has promised (Heb. 10:36).

January 5: Keeping Perspective

When I hear somebody sigh that life is hard,
I am tempted to ask, "Compared to what?"
—Sydney J. Harris

Israel escaped slavery in Egypt to travel through a desert with Moses, but hunger caused them to complain that they used to have it so good in Egypt. They forgot about the backbreaking work and their routine beatings, because at least they had meat and bread to eat (Exod. 16:3). Israel had no perspective of the Promised Land where Moses was taking them because they were living in a false, rosy image of the past. Our minds tend to work the same way. We choose to remember the good parts of our pasts but brush over the parts that were bad. Maybe it's a failed relationship or a job that didn't work out, but for whatever reason, we miss what never really was. The lesson for Israel is also true for us. It's hard to see the greater places we want to go if we're living in the rosy images we paint of our past.

But I focus on this one thing: Forgetting the past and looking forward to what lies ahead (Phil. 3:13 NLT).

January 6: Lifting Up Hands

I'll stand, arms high, and heart abandoned.
—Hillsong United

There are many ways to honor God with our worship, and one way is raising our hands in praise. When children want to be closer to their fathers, they raise their hands to be lifted out of their present circumstances. They desire the fulfillment of being closer to their father just as we desire to draw closer to our heavenly Father. When we lift our hands to our heavenly Father, He uplifts us.

Lift up your hands toward the sanctuary, and praise the LORD (Ps. 134:2 NLT).

January 7: Dreams and Divine Appointments

God is always preparing and positioning us for divine appointments. And prayer is the way we discern our next move.
—Mark Batterson

The dreams God has put in our hearts often do not come to fruition without His divine appointments. If we are staying at home and hoping for a miracle, that's not how God works. But it's also true that we should not go throughout our day without praying over our calendars, thoughtlessly accepting meetings without first being sensitive to the leading of the Holy Spirit. God's favor always flows through people, so if He has given us dreams, He will also provide divine appointments. We must trust Him to open the doors that no one can shut but also shut the doors we ought not to walk through. Let's pray over our calendars, asking God to lead us by the Holy Spirit so we can recognize divine appointments when God puts them in our lives.

The LORD says, "I will guide you along the best pathway for your life. I will advise you and watch over you" (Ps. 32:8 NLT).

January 8: Make Today Your Masterpiece

Make today your masterpiece.

—John Wooden

Whether it is a painter, writer, musician, or actor, artists love to produce art that will inspire and help others. Eventually, their art might earn them recognition, but oftentimes, that is not what motivates them to create art. Many artists produce art simply for the love of their craft, and it is what they feel called to do. For Christians who live a life of service and are generous to others, recognition may not ever come in this lifetime, but that should not be their motivation for living that way. Rather, may we decide that we will serve others and be generous simply because we are living out God's call to love Him and love people. By doing that, we make today our masterpiece.

Let us not love in word or talk but in deed and in truth (1 John 3:18 ESV).

January 9: **Leadership by Empowering Others**

Nothing is particularly hard if you divide it into small jobs.
—Henry Ford

Moses had a difficult time being the lone judge of Israel's court cases. Everybody—and I mean everybody—came to him for everything they had difficulty with. Eventually, judging alone became overwhelming. Moses's father-in-law told him he couldn't keep living this way. So his father-in-law organized a management system so that all the tasks Moses had done alone would be delegated to leaders subordinate to him. Arguably, this system saved Israel and freed their leader to do what he was called to do—hear from God and lead the people of Israel to the Promised Land. Likewise, if you want to successfully lead any organization, don't be the lone ranger that goes it all alone. That is unsustainable. Instead, exercise leadership by empowering others. You will be working with your head and not just your hands, and those following you will appreciate the new responsibility. Your organization will run more effectively.

You should also choose some of the people to be judges and leaders (Exod. 18:21 ERV).

January 10: **Being Open-Minded**

Always keep an open mind.
—Phil Jackson

In my first year at the University of Texas, I was paired with a roommate, Daniel, from Costa Rica. I assumed this Costa Rican wouldn't know anyone and that I'd let him hang out with me and the three people I knew at UT. To my surprise, Daniel already had tons and tons of Central and South American friends. Instead of him tagging along with me, I tagged along with him, and many of those people became my friends. I learned to appreciate the unique cultures of these diverse countries, and

I also learned this valuable life lesson: Sometimes it's the people we least expect who end up blessing us the most. Stay open to whatever God wants to do, and just watch as He brings the right people along to bless you.

Trust in the LORD *with all your heart, and do not lean on your own understanding* (Prov. 3:5 ESV).

January 11: Priority Check

Our greatest fear should not be of failure but of succeeding at things in life that don't really matter.

—Francis Chan

When we get to the end of our days, will we be able to say that we lived for the things that matter then? Most people on their deathbeds won't think, "I wish I'd worked more or I'd purchased a newer car or bigger house." Rather, they often look back with regrets that they didn't become reconciled or spend more time with their family or tell them, "I love you." They usually do not regret the chances they took but rather the ones they didn't take. They wish they would have had integrity when it cost them. These are the principles that make a successful life, and yet sometimes they're hard to live by. James 4:14 says, "What is your life? You are a mist that appears for a little while and then vanishes." We may think we have forever to get our priorities right, but actually, life will go by much faster than we think, so let's decide to make it our aim to get it right in this one life we have been given.

So that you may live a life worthy of the Lord and please him in every way: bearing fruit in every good work, growing in the knowledge of God (Col. 1:10).

January 12: **Laughing at Ourselves**

Angels can fly because they take themselves lightly,
devils fall because of their gravity.
—G. K. Chesterton

Abraham's wife, Sarah, was 89 years old and barren. Imagine Sarah's many years of disappointment and regret when she was unable to have a child. God revealed to Abraham that Sarah would have a child, but Sarah's initial reaction was to scoff and say something like, "Yeah right! I'm too old." One year later, God gave Sarah a baby, Isaac, and all she could do was laugh, saying, "God has made laughter for me; everyone who hears will laugh with me" (Gen. 21:6 ESV). Sarah learned to look at the events taking place in her life in proportion to God's greater plan and laugh at herself. Imagine someone old enough to be a great-grandma just had her first baby! God has a good sense of humor. Similarly, we must weigh the negative events transpiring in our lives in proportion to God's greater plan. You might not feel that way right now, but perhaps eventually you will look back and laugh, saying, "So that's what God was doing! That's funny."

God has made laughter for me; everyone who hears will laugh with me (Gen. 21:6 ESV).

January 13: **Visions Require Faith**

Pray as though everything depended on God.
Work as though everything depended on you.
—Saint Augustine

Our visions for our lives require faith. If our visions come easily and don't require faith, then our visions are too small. We must ask God to give us visions for our lives that are so big that the only way we can realize our visions is by the hand of an all-powerful God. It doesn't matter how hard we work. What matters is who will supernaturally provide in ways we would have never thought possible in the natural realm. Then, when circumstances arise on the way to realizing our visions, we will not be shaken because our hope is in a God who never fails. Let's ask God today to encourage us in our faith, so no matter what comes our way, our faith will be unshakable.

And whatever you ask in prayer, you will receive, if you have faith (Matt. 21:22 ESV).

January 14: God Never Sleeps

A dark cloud is no sign that the sun has lost his light; and dark black convictions are no arguments that God has laid aside His mercy.
—Charles Spurgeon

Scripture says that God's compassions or mercies "are new every morning" (Lam. 3:23). Whenever we battle sin, we may feel better about ourselves after we have repented and time passes, but I do not believe that "morning" should be taken literally. God never sleeps. He is working on our behalves 24/7. As soon as we make up our minds to start afresh—no matter how hard we have fallen or how little time has passed—by God's grace, we are free to get up and move forward.

If we confess our sins, he is faithful and just and will forgive us our sins and purify us from all unrighteousness (1 John 1:9).

January 15: **Words Matter**

God forbid that I should travel with anybody a quarter of an hour without speaking of Christ to them.
—George Whitefield

St. Francis of Assisi once said, "Preach the gospel at all times. When necessary, use words." This quote is right—we should preach the gospel by living in such a way that we are recognized for being loving, generous, and kind. But it is also ill-advised because we actually must use words to effectively share our faith with those who aren't in right relationship with Christ. Words matter. There are also non-Christians who are loving, generous, and kind, so these attributes alone do not always cause our friends to ask us about Christ. Preaching the gospel by how we live our lives must be accompanied by literally preaching the gospel with our words. Christ-centered conversations often do not happen unless we are willing to initiate these important conversations.

He [Jesus] said to them, "Go into all the world and preach the gospel to all creation (Mark 16:15).

January 16: **Harvest Time**

Always do your best. What you plant now, you will harvest later.
—Og Mandino

Have you ever thought to yourself, "I really thought that by now I would be further along than where I am"? Maybe you thought you would have accomplished the goals you'd set much earlier in your life or that the goals you did reach would have brought the desired outcome of happiness. We question whether God is pleased with us because sometimes we do not feel pleased with where and who we are. If you are doing your best to honor God, He is pleased with you! So stay faithful, and don't give up. Recognize that some trees do not bear fruit for many years. And likewise, we may not see the fruit of what we have sown immediately, but it might take many years or even decades to see the difference we have made. Sometimes, we may not realize it in this lifetime but in the next. God is working in us and through us whether we always see it or not.

Let us not grow weary of doing good, for in due season we will reap, if we do not give up (Gal. 6:9 ESV).

January 17: Showing God Gratitude

The art of acceptance is the art of making someone who has just done you a small favor wish that he might have done you a greater one.
—Martin Luther King, Jr.

God blesses us every day whether we realize it or not. The little things that many might take for granted—such as food on our tables, health in our bodies, roofs over our heads, and cars to get to work—are God's blessings. One of the best ways to show gratitude to God is to profess His goodness to everyone who will listen. That way, we thank Him by doing our part to fulfill the Great Commission.

I will praise you, LORD, with all my heart; I will tell of all the marvelous things you have done (Ps. 9:1 NLT).

January 18: Send Me, I'll Go!

God will take you out of your comfort zone, but he will never take you out of your sweet spot.
—Steven Furtick

Sometimes, we stay contained in our comfort zones, saying things such as "I can't afford it," "I don't have the time," or, if you're spiritual, "I'm not called to do that." Just outside your comfort zone is a bigger sphere to increase, a place to grow. God wants to take you there, and to do so, your attitude must be, "Send me, I'll go!" Let's pray today that we will be people who surrender our lives and dreams to pursue whatever it is God has called us to do.

> *Then I heard the voice of the Lord saying, "Whom shall I send? And who will go for us?" And I said, "Here am I. Send me! (Isa. 6:8).*

January 19: **Reacting Right**

> *You have to do your own growing no matter*
> *how tall your grandfather was.*
> —Abraham Lincoln

I was running through my neighborhood one evening, carefully watching for cars and wearing a bright neon safety vest so drivers could see me. I thought I'd protected myself well until all of a sudden, out of nowhere, a beast ran up and wildly barked at my heels. With haste, I anxiously jumped three feet before realizing the beast was a schnauzer! I honestly was tempted to get on all fours and show it my teeth, growl, sneer, and bark back to scare it away. As Christians, we are sometimes attacked undeservedly. Sometimes, our instinct is to react with our base nature and fight that person on their level. It's in those times that God allows circumstances to test us to see if we'll act and react in a Christ-like manner, standing tall, and staying the course.

> *Because you know that the testing of your faith produces perseverance* (James 1:3).

January 20: **Just Be You**

Your time is limited, so don't waste it living someone else's life.

—Steve Jobs

I've always loved African-American culture, and I still do. So in sixth grade, I wore a FUBU (For Us, By Us) jersey. I thought I was paying tribute to the African-American culture, but that day it seemed like everyone, both black and white, in my middle school mocked me and laughed at me! I learned a valuable lesson that day: you can admire other people, but you cannot be them, and they cannot be you. You just have to be you. That lesson is true at any season of life. Don't mimic the supermom you see on TV; don't make a big body builder's muscles your benchmark; don't make your father's success an indicator of your future. You are a custom design, a first edition, and thus there is nobody else like you. God has not called you to live out the script of someone else's life; He's called you to do your best and just be you. Pray today that you will be comfortable being exactly who God has called you to be.

For we are God's masterpiece. He has created us anew in Christ Jesus, so we can do the good things he planned for us long ago (Eph. 2:10 NLT).

January 21: **Exiting and Entering**

Every exit is an entry somewhere else.

—Tom Stoppard

Often a rejection can be hard to take, but could it be that that rejection is an invitation into something greater? Joseph's brothers not only rejected him, but they also sold him into slavery. And that led to his becoming second-in-command of all of Egypt. Eventually, he was in a unique position that God had ordained in order to save his entire family from starving during a famine that had struck their land. Joseph said to his brothers, "You intended to harm me, but God intended it for good"

(Gen. 50:20). Likewise, the unexpected layoff or abrupt end of a relationship may feel like a setback, but it could be God's setup for something greater for you. The stumbling block could be your stepping stone; an end is but a new beginning.

Forget the former things; do not dwell on the past. See, I am doing a new thing! (Isa. 43:18–19).

January 22: First Love

> *There's no love like the first.*
> —Nicholas Sparks

Do you remember the first time you met Jesus? Perhaps He was new and exciting. He became all you cared about, and you told your friends and family how much you loved Him. Maybe you said things like this: "I never want to sin again because of what Jesus did for me on the cross." Or maybe you said, "He is my source of joy, strength, and peace, so I never want to leave His presence." Jesus, however, doesn't just want to be your first love; He wants to be your last. Let us pray today that we would never lose this first love for Jesus so we can live a life filled with passion and purpose that He calls us to.

I am the Alpha and the Omega, the First and the Last, the Beginning and the End (Rev. 22:13).

January 23: Surrender

> *You cannot out-dream God.*
> —Rick Warren

Many people spend all their adult lives trying to fulfill the dreams of their youth. Today, I want to ask you to do something that will take audacious faith. Surrender every dream you have to God. "Here You go, God; here is my desire to receive earthly recognition, to love and be loved, and to achieve material success. I want You to empty me of every ambition I have because I trust that the life You have for me is greater than the life I could ever dream of. You are the potter, and I am the clay. God, I'm Yours." As Jesus said, "Seek first his kingdom and his righteousness, and all these things will be given to you" (Matt. 6:33). Surrender is not a one-time ordeal; it is a habit you will have to continue to do as God blesses you. Doing so means you live the life to become the Christian that God created you to be.

Whoever finds his [lower] life will lose it [the higher life], and whoever loses his [lower] life on My account will find it [the higher life] (Matt. 10:39 AMPC).

January 24: Christ's Strength

God's strength in your weakness is His presence in your life.
—Andy Stanley

We often rely on our own strength to accomplish what God has called us to do. Maybe it's our talents, abilities, resources, contacts, and self-determination. But there's something to be said about those who rely on God's strength. Scripture says, "I can do all things through Christ who strengthens me" (Phil. 4:13 NKJV). In Christ, we can overcome any sin, conquer any fear, grow like never before, and experience doors opened to us that no one can shut. To see a breakthrough, it takes a combination of doing what we can naturally do and God's help supernaturally to do what only He can do. Let's choose not to fight battles alone but rather allow God to fight for us.

I pray that out of his glorious riches he may strengthen you with power through his Spirit in your inner being (Eph. 3:16).

January 25: **A Balanced Perspective**

When you are courting a nice girl, an hour seems like a second. When you sit on a red-hot cinder, a second seems like an hour. That's relativity.
—Albert Einstein

What if we could weigh our problems in proportion with the rest of the world (about 7 billion people.) While one tired man prays he doesn't have to work late, another tired man prays he can find a job to feed his family. As one stressed mother wishes she had more time to herself to unwind, another stressed mother wishes she had more time with her terminally ill child. That doesn't mean that some of our problems are not legitimate; however, global relativity weighs our problems on a balanced scale.

Let me be weighed in an even balance that God may know mine integrity (Job 31:6 KJV).

January 26: **Catching a Fire**

Catch on fire with enthusiasm, and people will come for miles to watch you burn.
—John Wesley

There are events and circumstances—maybe it's a job loss, a divorce, the death of a loved one, a betrayal, a failed business—that zap our joy and zeal for life and leave us feeling broken, cynical, or burned out. Those events can be extremely difficult, and some pain and grieving are only natural for a season. However, God doesn't want us to stay in that place forever. At some point, we must ask God in prayer to fill us with His Spirit so a fire can be lit in us to live with godly passion and joy again. What we often find is that God will turn some of the most miserable times in our lives into ministries where we can help others and share the gospel.

Restore to me the joy of your salvation, and uphold me with a willing spirit (Ps. 51:12 ESV).

January 27: **Weeping Turns to Joy**

When things are bad, we take comfort in the thought that they could always get worse. And when they are, we find hope in the thought that things are so bad they have to get better.
—Malcolm S. Forbes

If you believe God can talk to you, then don't doubt the devil's capability. When you're going through something, the devil will tell you your situation will never end. He'll have you feeling helpless and hopeless. Know this: "There is a time for everything, and a season for every activity under the heavens" (Eccles. 3:1). Feelings change like seasons change; loneliness, doubt, and fear turn to comfort, assurance, and joy. The devil knows that if he can make your mind dark, you will find it harder to be the light of the world.

Weeping may stay for the night, but rejoicing comes in the morning (Ps. 30:5).

January 28: **Tie a Knot and Hang On**

When you come to the end of your rope, tie a knot and hang on.
—Franklin D. Roosevelt

Faith in its purest form requires strength to hang on when you're at the end of your rope. You may not feel quite right, or you may not feel anything for that matter. You may have been seeking the Lord's help for some time now, but He hasn't delivered yet. However, you know too much about Him to doubt Him because He's come through for you before. You may not have all the answers right now, but you trust the One who does. Tie the knot there, don't slip any further, and hang on. During those hard times in the past when you didn't have anything but God, He truly became your everything. God must become your everything again. God has never failed you, and He never will, so trust that He will deliver in His perfect timing.

> *But continue thou in the things which thou hast learned and hast been assured of, knowing of whom thou hast learned them* (2 Tim. 3:14 KJV).

January 29: Hearing and Doing

> *All right everyone, line up alphabetically according to your height.*
> —Casey Stengel

It's impossible to line up alphabetically according to height, but did you catch it the first time? Sometimes, we hear only what we want to hear. Some hear what God has said on a matter but fail to do it because they begin to rationalize it in their minds. "Well, this is a different time; there's no way He expects me not to do that." In effect, they have distorted God's Word. God's absolute truth is thus made relative according to our personal desires or life's contexts. Scripture says, "For if anyone is a hearer of the word and not a doer, he is like a man who looks intently at his natural face in a mirror. For he looks at himself and goes away and at once forgets what he was like" (James 1:23–24 ESV). Let us pray that we will honor and obey Jesus who is the same yesterday, today, and forever. He, like His Word, never changes.

> *Then He said to them, "Take heed what you hear. With the same measure you use, it will be measured to you; and to you who hear, more will be given* (Mark 4:24 NKJV).

January 30: **Private Victories**

Never deliberate about what is clearly wrong,
and try to persuade yourself that it is not.
—Frederick Temple

When football's finest players fight to the finish, one team is crowned champion, confetti falls, and fans crowd the streets. The victory is widely recognized by the public for weeks. The athletes can expect national press coverage, a city parade, and countless parties in their honor. On the contrary, when we are in spiritual warfare to overcome temptation, no confetti falls, no parties are thrown, and we usually don't even get a pat on the back when we win. So we may sometimes ask ourselves, "What's the point of fighting so hard? This win is a private victory. Only God and perhaps my inner circle know what I've gone through and overcome." However, when our hearts are pure and our minds are at peace, there isn't anything more gratifying than recognizing that God is smiling down on us for winning the battle.

For You, Lord, will bless the [uncompromisingly] righteous [him who is upright and in right standing with You]; as with a shield You will surround him with goodwill (pleasure and favor) (Ps. 5:12 AMPC).

January 31: **Purpose in Your Work**

It's not enough to have lived. We should be determined
to live for something.
—Winston S. Churchill

In 2015, I was hired to work on Ted Cruz's presidential campaign. I was 26 at the time, and my assignment was to travel the country campaigning with his 76-year-old father, Rafael. Over the course of the nine months of the campaign, we traveled the entire country, going to five or six meetings per day, sometimes in multiple states. Despite Rafael's age, which most would consider a reason to slow down, Rafael would sprint into the airport terminal from one flight to the next, and I would just try to keep up. He had more energy than most Millennials I know because he was so passionate about a purpose bigger than just living for himself or for the here and now. Although the campaign ended, our friendship did not. I have learned so much from Rafael, and I now consider him a mentor and best friend. I hope that one day when I am 76, I will be full of energy and still living life for a purpose much bigger than myself. Let us pray today that we will find and commit ourselves to work that energizes us and work in which we can find purpose.

*"For I know the plans I have for you," says the L*ORD*. "They are plans for good and not for disaster, to give you a future and a hope"* (Jer. 29:11 NLT).

February 1: **Praying Through**

If the devil can't make you bad, he'll make you busy.
—Christian Proverb

Imagine that you're a running back trying to pound the football into the end zone. You're prepared to run the play to score the winning touchdown. The football is handed off to you, and boom! The defense knocks you on your backside. When you pray, the devil plays defense, doing all he can to stop you from connecting with God. He will distract you by diverting your attention to everything else that you "need" to do today. Or better yet, you will be convinced that you're too busy to pray at all. May we put aside the distractions today to connect with God. There truly is nothing more important.

Be alert and of sober mind. Your enemy the devil prowls around like a roaring lion looking for someone to devour (1 Pet. 5:8).

February 2: **Pray in Faith**

Prayer is what moves God.

—Rex Johnson

If a football player does not believe his team can win, then all the practice he puts in every day feels like it is for nothing. If he doesn't practice hard enough or at all, then he becomes rusty and out of shape. If he doesn't know how to properly run a play, then he can't effectively move the offense forward. In that same manner, without true faith, your prayer life may devolve into a superstitious ritual. If you neglect to pray, then you become more prone to sin and out of sync with God. If you forget to pray, then you cannot expect God to move in your situation. Take time to connect with God today and watch as He comes through for you.

And whatever you ask in prayer, you will receive, if you have faith (Matt. 21:22 ESV).

February 3: **Receiving Criticism Well**

The trouble with most of us is that we'd rather be ruined by praise than saved by criticism.

—Norman Vincent Peale

God will often use the criticism of others to mold your character and make you more like Christ. It never feels good to hear ourselves described as selfish, greedy, or conceited, but we ought to reflect and assess whether or not these descriptions are true. There are times when people have ulterior motives for what they're saying, and they may be wrong. However, there are also times that they are spot-on even if they do have ulterior motives. Being able to receive criticism well is especially important when it's from people who are close to us. They probably have our best interests at heart. It takes both a growth mindset and humility for us to see criticism through this lens. So, may we pray that God will use criticism as an opportunity to mold us into His likeness.

The ear that listens to life-giving reproof will dwell among the wise (Prov. 15:31 ESV).

February 4: **Rest**

> *Sometimes the most important thing in a whole day is the rest*
> *we take between two deep breaths.*
> —Etty Hillesum

One day, Jesus and His disciples were on a boat when a colossal storm hit them. As the waves began to mount, the disciples were greatly distressed, but not Jesus. He was asleep! Jesus woke up to calm the storm but not before He made it a point to rest. Here's my point. If Jesus needed rest to carry out what He was called to do (and He's God), then so do we. Perhaps rest for us isn't sleeping but rather an activity that rejuvenates us. When we rest, really rest, we will be ready to face life's storms and do whatever God has called us to do.

Then Jesus said, "Let's go off by ourselves to a quiet place and rest awhile" (Mark 6:31 NLT).

February 5: **Just Like Dad**

> *I am very happy to say I look like my dad.*
> —James Blunt

People who have known my dad for a long time tell me that I'm starting to look like him. Through my eyes, I see more differences than similarities, but I always receive this as a compliment because I want to be like my dad. Likewise, when people look at us as Christians, we want them to say we are beginning to look like our heavenly Father—more loving, gracious, generous, compassionate, pure, patient, peaceful, and faithful. When people say something like that to you, your first tendency may be to brush it off because you see all the ways you're not like Him. But as you grow in your faith, you begin to look more like Him.

You must be holy because I, the LORD, am holy. I have set you apart from all other people to be my very own (Lev. 20:26 NLT).

February 6: **Planting Seeds**

Actions are the seed of fate. Deeds grow into destiny.
—Harry S. Truman

Every time you tell someone about Jesus, you are planting a seed. They may not quite know what to make of the seed yet, but one day, that seed can grow into a bountiful harvest. You may not be the one who brings in that harvest; God may decide to use someone else. But your action still brought forth heavenly fruit. Let us pray that we will be Christians who are actively planting seeds of hope, generosity, and love so God can bring forth a harvest.

So neither the one who plants nor the one who waters is anything, but only God, who makes things grow (1 Cor. 3:7).

February 7: **Courage**

Courage is not simply one of the virtues,
but the form of every virtue at the testing point.
—C. S. Lewis

Esther, a Jew, was chosen above every other woman in Persia to be King Ahasuerus's queen. The king's official, Haman, plotted to destroy the

Jews, telling the king that the Jews were disobedient to the king's law. The king empowered Haman to do as he pleased to the Jews, not knowing that his wife was Jewish. Under Persian law, nobody was allowed to disrupt the king's court unless they were called upon. If you did so anyway, you were risking your life. The only exception was the unlikely chance the king held out his scepter to spare the intruder's life. Mordecai told Esther that she must speak up because she was in that very position for such a time as this. Esther responded, "If I perish, I perish" (Esther 4:16). What Esther was saying was that she'd rather die for speaking up for her values than live and remain silent. Maybe we like to think of ourselves as good people with strong values who do what's right. Most of the time, that is likely true. But if we fail to act when we see injustice, if we keep silent when we hear racist comments, if we live apathetic to the oppressed, how righteous are we really? We mustn't put our values aside simply because it makes our lives easier.

Be strong and courageous. Do not be afraid or terrified because of them, for the LORD your God goes with you; he will never leave you nor forsake you (Deut. 31:6).

February 8: Just Smile

Peace begins with a smile.
—Mother Teresa

Sometimes, the entire world can feel as if it's crumbling around us; however, it's important that we smile through it anyway. That isn't saying we shouldn't be honest with how we are feeling whenever we're feeling low and find healthy ways to cope with life's adversities. It's saying that we control whether or not we smile. We cannot choose how people act toward us or what happens to us, but we can choose how we react to our situations. When we smile, regardless of whether our situations change right away, our attitude about our situations can begin to change immediately. Just smile.

If I say, "I will forget my complaint, I will put off my sad face, and be of good cheer" (Job 9:27 ESV).

February 9: Praying before Reading

There is more treasure in books than in all the pirate's loot on Treasure Island.
—Walt Disney

Do you want to grow in your faith and understanding? Pray this before delving into God's Word: "Lord, I need the Holy Spirit to lead me to what it is I need to learn. As I read today, bestow upon me golden revelation, so I draw closer to You. In Jesus's name. Amen." By looking at your devotion time in the Word as a treasure hunt, you are sure to find gems that could otherwise have gone unnoticed.

Cry out for insight, and ask for understanding. Search for them as you would for silver; seek them like hidden treasures (Prov. 2:3–4 NLT).

February 10: Loving Lizzy

Some of us think holding on makes us strong; but sometimes it is letting go.
—Hermann Hesse

When I was eight years old, I walked into the pet store and bought the cutest of them all—a lady lizard that I named Lizzy. I did everything with her. She met my parents, she met my friends, and we went on long walks. I made sure I provided for her as best I could. I spent hours hunting down and bringing her the most delicious crème de la crème of crickets. She would always eat them, but I never heard her say thank you. I'd pet her affectionately, but because she was a reptile, she was incapable of reciprocating my affection. At an early age, I learned a valuable life lesson, not just about lizards but also about people. Some people are incapable of loving us the way we deserve. If you're the one investing everything—always picking up the tab, driving long distances, helping with others' problems—and your personal concerns fall on deaf ears, then most likely you're in a parasitic relationship. I'm not saying that there aren't times you shouldn't help people, but if a person in your life cares only for themselves, it's time to reconsider the relationship. If you stay in a parasitic relationship when you don't have to, then, like a vampire, that person will suck the life out of you. Get out! Let vampires keep on sucking, but just don't let it be on you.

There are "friends" who destroy each other, but a real friend sticks closer than a brother (Prov. 18:24 NLT).

February 11: **Wrath and Love**

I have always found that mercy bears richer fruits than strict justice.
—Abraham Lincoln

In fourth grade, I had two teachers, Mrs. Borque and Mrs. Horseradish (name changed). Together they were an unlikely pair—day and night, sweet and sour, good cop and bad cop. Both teachers were effective in taming a loud and lively class. Mrs. Borque was so nice that her class wanted to obey her, but Mrs. Horseradish was so mean that her class feared what would happen if we disobeyed her. Similarly, there are two opposing views of God's nature. One is a merciful and gracious being, and the other is a just and wrathful God. One view of God's nature espouses love, and the other causes fear, and both are supported in scripture. Experiencing the wrath of Mrs. Horseradish made me appreciate the grace of Mrs. Borque all the more. While fear of God sometimes keeps us on the straight and narrow (Prov. 9:10), the love of God causes us to want to be our best and be an extension of His love.

On some have compassion, making a distinction; but others save with fear (Jude 1:22–23 NKJV).

February 12: **Friends of God**

Friendship is unnecessary, like philosophy, like art. . . . It has no survival value; rather it is one of those things which give value to survival.
—C. S. Lewis

Sometimes friendship can seem like a revolving door. People say they will always be there for you, and then all of a sudden and maybe with no warning, they're nowhere to be found. God, however, is always there. Even when we've been faithless to Him and taken Him for granted, He remains faithful and is always there for us. Nothing can change God's agape love for us. His love endures forever. It's truly special when we do find lifelong friends, but there is no friendship as sweet as an eternity with God in heaven.

He was called a friend of God (James 2:23 ESV).

February 13: **A Journey with Purpose**

A journey is like marriage. The certain way to be wrong is to think you control it.
—John Steinbeck

When we're truly in a relationship with Jesus, we are no longer the ones in control of our journeys. We must do three things scripture says on this: (1) trust the Lord with all our hearts, (2) lean not on our own understanding, and (3) submit to Him in all our ways. When we follow His Word, God will direct our paths. Jesus may take us to places we weren't expecting on our journeys, but ultimately, we will find that His purpose for our journey is so much greater than the journey we would have had on our own.

Help me to accomplish the purpose of my journey (Gen. 24:12 TLB).

February 14: Accepting God's Love

Let us always meet each other with smile,
for the smile is the beginning of love.
—Mother Teresa

My sister, Nina, and her boyfriend, Jon, dated for more than two years without ever saying they loved each another. Jon wanted to wait for the right time. On a cruise ship game show, of all places, he got down on one knee and said, "Nina, I love you. Will you marry me?" Soon after, they were married and have been ever since. Likewise, Christians have access to God's love by virtue of Christ's death and resurrection. Imagine Jesus down on one knee also popping the question, "Will you marry me?" Doing so means you accept His love and belong to Him for an eternity in heaven. Christ is referred to as the bridegroom, and the church is His bride for whom He will return one day. The most beautiful thing about this picture is that you are never alone with Christ's love because you have the Holy Spirit inside of you. Maybe some of you need to accept Christ's love for the first time. Others may need to rekindle their relationship with Him. This Valentine's Day, will you accept Christ's love?

I have been crucified with Christ. It is no longer I who live, but Christ who lives in me. And the life I now live in the flesh I live by faith in the Son of God, who loved me and gave himself for me (Gal. 2:20 ESV).

February 15: **Belief and Faith**

We are never defeated unless we give up on God.
—Ronald Reagan

Too often people give all they think they can give and fail to have faith in God for what He can do. They don't truly believe in the power of God even though they might say they do. Science tells you to trust in what you see, but faith tells you to trust in what you cannot see. Believe God for a miracle. When you do everything you naturally can, then trust God to do the supernatural. Give 100 percent, and from there, God will exceed all expectations by meeting you at 101 percent.

That your faith might not rest in the wisdom of men but in the power of God (1 Cor. 2:5 ESV).

February 16: **Taking Risks and Enlarging Territory**

The biggest risk is not taking any risk. . . . In a world that is changing really quickly, the only strategy that is guaranteed to fail is not taking risks.
—Mark Zuckerberg

God knows the distances we are truly capable of going, and it is usually further than what we initially are comfortable with. Stepping out in faith often means we must step outside of our comfort zones. We cannot enlarge our territories if we do not. We have to assume risk to reap rewards, and opportunities have a shelf life, so they must be seized at the right time. We cannot wait forever. We have to move. Today, let's prayerfully trust God and refuse to be afraid to go the distance to expand our territory. Whatever direction God is calling us to go, we know that He will go before us and that He will never leave us.

Oh, that you would bless me and enlarge my territory! (1 Chron. 4:10).

February 17: God's Workmanship

Comparison is the death of joy.
—Mark Twain

I was four years old, and my little sister, Nina, was three. Unfortunately, she beat me both in learning to tie her shoes and in riding a bike. I felt like Esau when Jacob stole his birthright and his blessing, so in both instances I frantically learned to tie my shoes and ride a bike the same day she did. Perhaps I needed a push, but how often in life do we allow others' strengths to be the standard we wrongfully compare ourselves to? It probably happens all too often. Should a world-class bass player compare himself to the top band's lead singer? No. So you shouldn't compare something you're just okay at to another person's strength, or your joy will be snatched away. God knew exactly what He was doing when He made you with all the talents and abilities you possess. And He did so to accomplish a purpose in and through you. You are perfect just the way you are.

I praise you, for I am fearfully and wonderfully made (Ps. 139:14 ESV).

February 18: Nothing Is Impossible

To one who has faith, no explanation is necessary. To one without faith, no explanation is possible.
—Thomas Aquinas

In the natural, we can only do what is possible; however, faith requires an expectation that God can supernaturally do what is otherwise impossible. We must remember that nothing is too hard for God. Just a little bit of faith can instantly change both your outlook for the day and your long-term outcome of a trial, so imagine what God could do if we asked Him to increase the measure of our faith tenfold. Our God can mend any wound, heal any disease, provide for any financial need, restore broken relationships, and perform any miracle. We can call on God for anything, so let's go to Him with the expectation of a miracle. Let us pray today that we will have faith in God to truly believe, "For nothing will be impossible with God" (Luke 1:37 ESV).

Behold, I am the LORD, the God of all flesh. Is anything too hard for me? (Jer. 32:27 ESV).

February 19: My Will or Thy Will

Outside of Christ, I am weak; in Christ, I am strong.
—Watchman Nee

All too often, we impatiently try to force situations into happening our way rather than waiting on God to allow Him to do it His way. By doing it our way, we inevitably get ahead of God, and sometimes, there's danger pursuing something too soon that we aren't ready for or that isn't God's will for us at all. Perhaps it's a platform, an opportunity, or a relationship, and we set ourselves up for failure. That is not to say that we should be apprehensive in pursuit of all God has for us. But we should check our hearts and scripture to ensure we are in lockstep with the Holy Spirit, listening for wherever God may be calling us. Our attitudes ought to be ones of submission to God's greater will, wanting Him to close every path that He knows we should avoid and open only the paths that He wants us to explore.

Humble yourselves, therefore, under God's mighty hand, that He may lift you up in due time (1 Pet. 5:6).

February 20: **A Picturesque Vision**

A vision is a picture of your preferred future.
—Miles McPherson

It is important that we create a mental picture of what success looks like to us, or we may not like where we end up. That may sound silly to some, but take it a step further and literally put a picture on the wall or mirror of your personal goals, dreams, and pursuits. Pray, and then write things down in your journal. Rip out that page and put it on your wall or mirror to look at every day. God wants to give us the desires of our hearts, and if our hearts' desires are to bring Him glory, then He is pleased with us as we embark on bringing our visions to fruition.

Where there is no prophetic vision the people cast off restraint, but blessed is he who keeps the law (Prov. 29:18 ESV).

February 21: **When Faith Starts**

Faith starts at the point of human limitation.
—T. D. Jakes

Have you ever noticed that you never pray about things in your capacity to perform? You don't petition God for help getting out of bed, dressing yourself, or turning on the faucet to brush your teeth or make your coffee. If the bigger things you petitioned God for also came this easy, then faith would be futile. These bigger things that we petition God for—His help in writing a book, starting a business, planting a church, running for office, raising money to build water wells, beginning a marriage, or adopting a child—challenge us to trust in God's ability rather than rely solely on our own. When learning how to walk, babies must trust a parent to catch them when they stumble. Likewise, we must trust our heavenly Father to catch us as we learn how to walk by faith. Over time, a child's muscles grow strong enough to walk, and so do our faith muscles. What we often find is that the process of building our faith is just as rewarding as answered prayer.

Do not be anxious about anything, but in every situation, by prayer and petition, with thanksgiving, present your requests to God (Phil. 4:6).

February 22: **Worship Wins the War**

We must never rest until everything inside us worships God.
—A. W. Tozer

While Moses and Israel sojourned to the Promised Land, the Amalekite army attacked them. Moses instructed his protégé, Joshua, to take Israel to war with the Amalekites. But winning depended on Moses keeping his hands raised in worship on the mountaintop. If he grew weary and let his hands down, they began to lose. Notice that Moses didn't raise his hands after Israel won but while they were still fighting. So, despite how bleak a circumstance appears, keep worshiping God with all your might, and don't let up. Remember that there are people depending on you; God is fighting for you, and wars are won whenever you worship.

And please God by worshiping him with holy fear and awe (Heb. 12:28 NLT).

February 23: **When the Shoe Doesn't Fit**

I still have my feet on the ground, I just wear better shoes.
—Oprah Winfrey

As the expression goes, "If the shoe fits, wear it." I was at a sandal shop in Israel, looking to buy a pair. I tried a sandal on my right foot, and before I could try on the sandal for my left foot, I'd already bought them. Love at first sight, or so I thought! I decided to wear my shoes out of the store, but as I put on the left sandal, I realized it didn't fit. The more I walked, the more uncomfortable I became. By now, I regretted my impulse purchase. Someone said, "Maybe you just need to wear them in." I didn't think so. At first glance, the sandals looked right, and others agreed that the sandals perfectly suited me, but I knew that something just didn't feel right. Fortunately, the shoes were refundable; however, some life decisions are not. The obvious lesson is this: Don't make impulse purchases. There is, however, a deeper lesson: Don't let others decide what is right for you. When the shoe doesn't fit, don't continue to wear it if you don't have to.

Then the Lord said to him, "Take off the sandals from your feet" (Acts 7:33 ESV).

February 24: Richest Man in the Cemetery

Being the richest man in the cemetery doesn't matter to me.
Going to bed at night saying we've done something wonderful,
that's what matters to me.

—Steve Jobs

Pop culture has much to say about what makes a man or a woman. Society says to be handsome or beautiful, rich, famous, or powerful. While none of these attributes are inherently evil, Jesus called each of us to life more abundantly. That doesn't necessarily mean materially but rather emotionally and spiritually. We must not just live our lives for the here and now but with eternity in mind. Today, let's check whether our ambitions are rooted in the world or in the Word. One lands you in a coffin, and the other always leads you to the cross.

For what shall it profit a man, if he shall gain the whole world, and lose his own soul? (Mark 8:36 KJV).

February 25: **Experience God in Nature**

Nature is the art of God.

—Dante Alighieri

In 2019, I set out to check off a bucket list item by going to the world's seventh continent, Antarctica. I called a few of my friends to see if they could go with me, but for whatever reason, the answer was always no. I figured I might not get another chance in life to go unless I did it then, so I went for it. I first flew to Ushuaia, Argentina, and took an expedition cruise boat down to Antarctica. I made a ton of new friends along the way from many different countries I may not have connected with had I not traveled alone. As for being in Antarctica, it's hard to say what my favorite part was—having fun planting my Texas flag in the Antarctic snow, canoeing the most scenic sea, freezing my butt off by jumping in that sea, enjoying the sunset among the mountains, playing with penguins and whale watching—it was like stepping into a National Geographic magazine. The pictures I took really don't do Antarctica justice for how amazing the continent is. One of the ways I rest and reconnect with God is by spending time in nature, so I feel so blessed to have been able to make this amazing voyage. Being in nature is good for the soul. The lesson for me is also true for you in that we've got to find places to go that rejuvenate us and give us rest. So next time you're able to take a trip, I recommend going somewhere outdoors and beautiful, and going alone if you have to! In my experience, it may actually be better that way.

In his hand are the depths of the earth, and the mountain peaks belong to him. The sea is his, for he made it, and his hands formed the dry land (Psalm 95:4–5).

February 26: **Pursuing God**

Affection is responsible for nine-tenths of whatever solid and durable happiness there is in our lives.

—C. S. Lewis

When a man pursues a woman, wins her heart, and marries her, he cannot expect to have a healthy relationship with her by "having" her. He must continue pursuing his wife throughout their lives together. Likewise, whenever we pursue Jesus, get saved, and enter into a relationship with Him, we can't expect to have a healthy relationship with Him just by "having" Him. A relationship with Jesus is never static. A relationship is either declining or growing. We must continue pursuing Jesus throughout our lives. If for any reason our relationship with Jesus has been on a decline, let us pray that we would renew ourselves with the One who remains faithful.

God is faithful, who has called you into fellowship with his Son, Jesus Christ our Lord (1 Cor. 1:9).

February 27: **Sharing Jesus**

Americans will respect your beliefs if you just keep them private.

—Bill O'Reilly

Politics and religion are said to be best left out of dinner conversations because you do not want to risk offending anyone. Here's something to consider. Jesus very often offended people. Never did He keep His beliefs private because the salvation of the world was all too important. His ideology divided families. Political and religious elites hated Him and made Him somewhat of a polarizing figure. None of this stopped Him. Today, let's pray for courage to share the good news that Jesus has come to save the world.

For I am not ashamed of the gospel, because it is the power of God that brings salvation to everyone who believes (Rom. 1:16).

February 28: The Name of Jesus

I am not interested in power for power's sake, but I'm interested in power that is moral, that is right and that is good.
—Martin Luther King, Jr.

God is sovereign. So as a child of God, you have power in the name of Jesus! Call on Him anytime and anywhere. He can move mountains and make demons tremble. How much more, then, does He rule supreme over negative thoughts and dire circumstances? By the power of the Holy Spirit, you have authority in the name of Jesus. Let God intervene by calling on Him.

"What sort of new teaching is this?" they asked excitedly. "It has such authority! Even evil spirits obey his orders!" (Mark 1:27 NLT).

March 1: Friends Speak Life

Don't take counsel of your fears or naysayers.
—Colin Powell

There will always be people, even so-called friends, who will tell you that you cannot do something. Maybe they genuinely do not see the potential that God sees in you. Or worse, maybe they see it but hope you fail so you will stay at their level. After all, your success would only highlight their deficiencies and inadequacies. Either way, they actively work against you. By way of the Holy Spirit, God gives you spiritual discernment to be able to recognize who your true friends are, the ones who have your best interests at heart. A sign of a true friend is someone who breathes life, hope, future, faith, and God into your dreams. Choose to take counsel from the people who truly love and care for you. Ignore and cut off the rest.

There are "friends" who destroy each other, but a real friend sticks closer than a brother (Prov. 18:24 NLT).

March 2: Embracing Multiculturalism

Isn't it amazing that we are all made in God's image, and yet there is so much diversity among his people?
—Desmond Tutu

Paul, a Jew, was called to the Gentiles. Paul had so much to offer others that there's no way it could just be for people who looked like him, thought like him, and spoke like him. Instead, he went to Arabia, Syria, and Greece and embraced the diversity in their cultures. It's no wonder Paul had a multicultural group of friends. Some people today are too comfortable hanging out with their homogenous group of friends who have the same skin color, religion, or socioeconomic background. Don't just be tolerant of others; be intentional about making friends with people who are different from you. Be a connoisseur of cultures right in your own city. Experience new food, music, and traditions, and watch as your life becomes more richly blessed.

I am made all things to all men, that I might by all means save some (1 Cor. 9:22 KJV).

March 3: Nourish Your Soul

You can't enjoy life if you aren't nourishing your body.
—Tracy Gold

Sometimes, we eat healthy food, not knowing all the good it's doing in our bodies. It enables us to think more acutely and move in a more agile manner. However, if we splurge on sweets and neglect to nourish our bodies for even one day, we feel terrible physically. Sometimes, we can do what's right, not knowing all the good it's doing spiritually. That often enables us to hear God's voice and inherit His blessings. However, if even for a day we splurge in sin and neglect, we feel terrible spiritually. Let's decide today that we will nourish our souls with prayer and God's Word so we can continue to grow to be all God has created us to be.

Then Jesus explained, "My nourishment comes from doing the will of God, who sent me, and from finishing his work" (John 4:34 NLT).

March 4: Spiritual Warfare

You may have to fight a battle more than once to win it.
—Margaret Thatcher

Spiritual warfare. There are times we must fight with everything in us to stay the course Jesus has set for our lives. Some mornings, we may find ourselves looking in the mirror and giving ourselves a pep talk. We might say, "Listen here, this is how it's going down today." Do this over and over, and we begin to string together one good day after another. Eventually, we have momentum, but we cannot let up. On those occasions when we inevitably mess up (and though we will never be perfect), we must get back on track and strive for a general pattern of holiness so that how we live will bring glory to God.

Do not be overcome by evil, but overcome evil with good (Rom. 12:21 NKJV).

March 5: **Works and Righteousness**

Come live with me and be my love, and we will some new pleasures prove, of golden sands, and crystal beaches, with silken lines and silver hooks.

—John Donne

Righteousness is a by-product of our love for God like works are a by-product of our faith in God. However, we cannot properly fulfill love without righteousness, just as we cannot fulfill faith without works. Both are as interdependent as they are interconnected. Love is a commitment to God that we must fulfill every day because ultimately, we love Him not by what we say but by what we do. Day after day becomes the process of a lifetime in which we defy the gravitation to our default state of selfishness to pursue a life lived in the Holy Spirit of selflessness.

If you love me, keep my commands (John 14:15).

March 6: **Wake Up**

Hope is the dream of a waking man.

—Aristotle

If you weren't dreaming already, then you were sleepwalking. You are asleep to the unique talents and abilities God has blessed you with. You have an incredible opportunity since there is only one you in the entire world, and God created you with a purpose in mind. You are here to grow in your talents and abilities so you can glorify Him in the greatest way imaginable. For those awake, I hope you do not allow anyone or any circumstance to send you into hibernation. For those asleep, wake up and start dreaming.

Wake up, sleeper, rise from the dead, and Christ will shine on you (Eph. 5:14).

March 7: **Running Your Race**

Even if you're on the right track, you'll get run over if you just sit there.
—Will Rogers

I tactfully placed each footstep to avoid stumbling over sharp rocks and jagged roots. I leaped over a running stream to avoid being swept away, and I plowed through thick mud and cold wind that slowed my stride. The Mountain 5K was off to a good start, but then a competitor in front of me slipped and fell, and I piled over him. In life, sometimes we fall for reasons outside our control, and then we're left with two choices. We can sit there and fret or get up and finish. I picked myself up and finished my race, and I hope you will finish yours as well whenever you fall. We often cannot control how others choose to treat us or all the circumstances that happen to us, but we can always control how we choose to react to those people and circumstances.

And let us run with perseverance the race marked out for us (Heb. 12:1).

March 8: **One Step at a Time**

Success demands singleness of purpose.
—Vince Lombardi

Have you ever been so focused on the future that you failed to fully invest yourself in the present? While rock climbers glimpse to see what's ahead, they must watch every step to continue moving. To eventually realize God's long-term purpose in our lives, we must live out our purpose today. Let us pray that we will not overlook where God has placed us now. Today matters just as much as tomorrow.

Many plans are in a man's mind, but it is the Lord's purpose for him that will stand (Prov. 19:21 AMPC).

March 9: **No Limits**

I am realistic—I expect miracles.

—Wayne Dyer

There are times when we are guilty of limiting God, but this doesn't change that our God is limitless. The reality is that there isn't anything too hard for God. He wants to accomplish great things in our lives, but miracles require faith in Him and an expectation of Him. We choose every day either how little or how much faith we will have in God. In that way, we determine how far our faith takes us. We must reset our perceptions of reality to expect the miraculous.

For nothing will be impossible with God (Luke 1:37 ESV).

March 10: **Big Doors**

Big doors swing on little hinges.

—W. Clement Stone

Are you waiting for a door to open for you? God's blessing is sometimes not dependent on anything but your faith; just a little faith can open a big door. God is always home, and He wants to give good gifts to His children. Keep knocking with the expectation that God will answer. In due time, He will. Let us pray that we will be resilient not to give up knocking as God has called us to.

Keep on knocking, and the door will be opened to you (Matt. 7:7 NLT).

March 11: Fighting Materialism

It's not the daily increase but daily decrease.
Hack away at the unessential.

—Bruce Lee

We live in a culture of excess, whether it's the food we eat or the clothes we buy. Some say, "If I can just make a little more money to buy a bigger house or more expensive car, then I'll be happy." These temporary pleasures are not inherently wrong, but the pursuit of happiness for some is hedonistic. As Christians, we must make every effort to empty our lives of excess so when there is less of us, there will be more room for Jesus. God then fills us with love, joy, peace, patience, kindness, goodness, faithfulness, gentleness, and self-control.

He must increase, but I must decrease (John 3:30 NKJV).

March 12: Daily Worship

It's only when men begin to worship that they begin to grow.
—Calvin Coolidge

What if we went to the gym just once per week and tried to get a week's worth of exercise? It would be much harder to grow physically stronger. Similarly, we don't have to wait to worship God until church on Sunday when we're in front of a praise band. It is much harder to grow spiritually stronger that way. Worship of God isn't just a gesture of raised hands done weekly but a posture of our hearts through which we give Him adoration daily. When we meditate on Jesus throughout our days, we become what He created us to be, and He strengthens us.

God is Spirit, and those who worship Him must worship in spirit and truth (John 4:24 NKJV).

March 13: **Blind Spots**

Those who don't love you will tell you what you want to hear;
those who love you will lead you to the truth.
—Mother Teresa

Balaam set off on his donkey to meet the Moabite king. This meeting was in direct contrast to God's will, so God put an invisible angel on Balaam's path to punish him. Fortunately for Balaam, his donkey saw the angel when his master could not. Three times, the donkey did everything it could to evade the angel, and three times Balaam beat it. Like a scene from the movie *Shrek*, the donkey said, "What did I do to deserve this?" It became clear to Balaam that the donkey saw something he could not. When Balaam could finally see the angel, he informed Balaam that the donkey had spared his life. God often puts people in our lives to help us see the blind spots we're oblivious to or, worse, that we don't want to see. When they dare to let us know about what they see, it may be our natural tendency to lash out at them. But we must remember that we need people who love us enough to tell us, "The road you're on is dangerous. Stop! Turn around."

A brother is born to help in time of need (Prov. 17:17 NLT).

March 14: **Call Out**

The loneliest moment in life is when you have just experienced
that which you thought would deliver the ultimate,
and it has just let you down.
—Ravi Zacharias

There may come an hour when you ask, "Why is this happening to me?" Then you might say, "Where is God?" We may feel as if God isn't there for us, but He is always with us; He is there whenever we cry out to Him. God manifests Himself as the Father who picks up His child after a fall. He is the light that leads the lost through the dark. He is the whisperer welcoming the wanderer home. No matter what we go through in life, our God is our very present help. Whenever we call on His name, He will answer.

But if from there you seek the LORD your God, you will find him if you seek him with all your heart and with all your soul (Deut. 4:29).

March 15: **No Condemnation**

Thou wilt enjoy tranquility if thy heart condemn thee not.
—Thomas à Kempis

What is the difference between conviction and condemnation? Conviction is from God, and condemnation is from the enemy. God convicts us of our sin in a moment of weakness, but the enemy seeks to condemn us long after God has forgiven us. We must be able to recognize the difference, because if we fail to do that, we deny ourselves the joy and peace that God so freely gives. Moreover, we give the enemy victory over us. If we've repented of our sins to seek forgiveness from God and from the people we've offended, and if we've changed and become a better person, then God has forgiven us. Don't condemn yourself. Forgive yourself, and then go and enjoy a life filled with the joy and peace of God.

There is therefore now no condemnation to them which are in Christ Jesus, who walk not after the flesh, but after the Spirit (Rom. 8:1 KJV).

March 16: **Don't Worry about Tomorrow**

The best thing about the future is that it comes only one day at a time.
—Abraham Lincoln

Do you ever get caught up worrying about the future? Maybe you wonder if you'll ever get married or if you will be able to have children.

Maybe you imagine failing in business or being let go or becoming sick and not having enough money for retirement. Jesus said, "Can any one of you by worrying add a single hour to your life?" (Matt. 6:27). Jesus knew that worrying never helps and only hurts. So what's the alternative? Jesus pointed out that this life is more than just what we eat and drink, the clothes we wear, the cars we drive, and where we live. We must choose to seek His kingdom and His righteousness, trusting God that "all these things will be given to you as well" (Matt. 6:33). Let's decide today to take a deep breath, and one day at a time, we must let go of worry and replace it with a firmer grasp of and trust in Him.

Therefore do not worry about tomorrow, for tomorrow will worry about itself. Each day has enough trouble of its own (Matt. 6:34).

March 17: **Strategy and Faith**

Christians set up a false dichotomy between trusting God and strategy.
—Mike Tilley

What if life could be reduced to a crossroads of allowing life to happen to us and making life happen? Strategy without faith leaves us trying to do everything on our own; faith without strategy leaves God scratching His head wondering how He can use us. Strategy plus faith prepares us to expect God's best. May we ask God today to give us a strategy to carry out whatever He has called us to do and the faith to trust that He will deliver.

A wise man thinks ahead; a fool doesn't, and even brags about it! (Prov. 13:16 TLB).

March 18: **Attempting Great Things**

Expect great things from God; attempt great things for God.
—William Carey

You may be uncertain about whether you can accomplish whatever it is you are called to do, but you cannot accomplish what you do not attempt. So just go for it. Do whatever your "it" is for God. There are some things we can't do alone, but with God, all things are possible. Seize your opportunity to grow and be blessed. Seek and serve God with all your heart, and He will see you through. There are no ifs, ands, or buts about it! Pray today that God will give you the courage and resolve to carry out whatever your "it" is.

And now, Lord, what do I wait for and expect? My hope and expectation are in you (Ps. 39:7 AMPC).

March 19: **Be a Minister**

Let every man abide in the calling wherein he is called and his work will be as sacred as the work of the ministry. It is not what a man does that determines whether his work is sacred or secular, it is why he does it.
—A. W. Tozer

Should we devote our lives to ministry or provide for our families? The short answer is both. God does not distinguish between the sacred and the secular, so whether we are in missions or marketing, whether we are a preacher or a politician, we are all called to minister to the physical and spiritual needs of others so they eventually come to a saving faith in Jesus. Let us ask God to show us how we can minister, no matter what our job titles are, so others can come to know Jesus and we can bring glory to Him.

And you will be called priests of our LORD, you will be named ministers of our God (Isa. 61:6).

March 20: Finding Inspiration for a Vision

When I think of vision, I have in mind the ability to see above and beyond the majority.

—Chuck Swindoll

There is a proverb that says, "Necessity is the mother of invention." Innovators pinpoint the needs of others even when people don't yet know what they need. They formulate a vision for something that does not yet exist to meet those needs. A vision does not always come by way of a loud, life-altering moment. Sometimes, inspiration is found over time by way of many conversations, books, podcasts, and other sources that begin to form an impression on our hearts. Moreover, God doesn't always give us a vision by stopping us in our tracks with an epic blinding light as He did with the Apostle Paul. Sometimes, God gives us a vision in the seemingly ordinary moments of life while we are doing something else. Other times, our eyes begin to open when we get away to still and quiet places of nature. When we pray, let's pray that God will give us a vision beyond what we can physically see.

Where there is no vision, the people perish (Prov. 29:18 KJV).

March 21: Puzzle Pieces

A good puzzle, it's a fair thing. Nobody is lying.
It's very clear, and the problem depends just on you.

—Erno Rubik

Each Christian in the church is like a different puzzle piece that God uses to bring Himself glory. Only God can place the puzzle pieces where they fit. Individually, we each bring something different to the table; together, we each fit in some special way to complete God's grander picture. There are beauty and harmony when we work with another for

God's good. Let us pray today that we will find exactly where we fit into God's picture so we are used for His purpose.

May the God of endurance and encouragement grant you to live in such harmony with one another, in accord with Christ Jesus, that together you may with one voice glorify the God and Father of our Lord Jesus Christ (Rom. 15:5–6 ESV).

March 22: Judge Not

If you judge people, you have no time to love them.
—Mother Teresa

Instead of judging people for the way they choose to live or trying to change them, what if we simply love them for exactly who they are and where they're at on their spiritual journey? As Jesus said, we might be judging someone for the speck in their eye when we have a plank in ours (Matt. 7:3). In other words, what we do not like about them—the self-promoting attention-seeking or whatever—may be much less important than our own faults. Maybe we are actually further along than they are in areas where we have strengths and they have obvious weaknesses. But so what! God is their judge, not us. It's our duty as Christians to love people who are difficult to love by treating them with kindness, generosity, and patience so God can begin to work on their hearts in His timing. In the meantime, He's interested in curbing the self-righteousness in ours.

Don't pick on people, jump on their failures, criticize their faults— unless, of course, you want the same treatment (Matt. 7:1 MSG).

March 23: **Intolerable Impressing**

Get someone else to blow your horn and the sound will carry twice as far.
—Will Rogers

When I was 13 years old, I rode my bike everywhere. One day, I noticed a pretty girl outside on her lawn, so naturally, I poked out my chest, flexed my arms, looked over at her, and kept looking back even as I passed her. As soon as I did, I rammed right into a fire hydrant and dove onto the concrete pavement. I blinked back the tears as I took an inventory of my scrapes and wounds. Then I humbly and swiftly got back on my bike. The lesson I learned was simple. Sometimes, when we try too hard to impress people, we make ourselves look foolish. We don't need to give a rundown of our résumé or a full account of your accomplishments when we want to impress somebody. Sometimes, after you hang out with someone just a short while, you recognize that they are high caliber, they have a strong character, they are going places, or they have been places. No words are necessary, and they need no introduction. We just know. One more point. You become far more impressive to others when you take a genuine interest in them rather than trying to get them to take an interest in you.

Let another praise you, and not your own mouth; a stranger, and not your own lips (Prov. 27:2 ESV).

March 24: **Preaching through Our Struggles**

The anecdote to the devil's temptation is the affirmation of the Father.
—Steven Furtick

The pastor who preaches against lust or greed also faces the temptation, again and again. The counselor who guides another through depression also confronts the same issues. Often what we struggle with most is what we preach best. Try it. It's more real that way because we have the experience. When we serve God, even through sin, hurt, and pain, Jesus reminds us that He is our remedy. Our misery can become our ministry.

If anyone serves, they should do so with the strength God provides, so that in all things God may be praised through Jesus Christ (1 Pet. 4:11).

March 25: **Going Places**

> *God will meet you where you are in order to take you where He wants you to go.*
> —Tony Evans

Aren't you grateful for a God who uses imperfect people for His purposes? God will take us just as we are with our hang-ups and screw-ups. He will humble and correct us if He has to. Our Lord will allow circumstances and bring people into our lives who will encourage us—all so He can put us exactly where we need to be in the center of His will. If you're frustrated today that you're still battling some of the same issues you have not gotten past yet, just recognize that God can still use you in spite of you to bring Himself glory. God can restore what was lost, raise to life the dreams we thought were dead, and heal the brokenness in us to give us new hope and a future in Him.

But those who hope in the Lord will renew their strength. They will soar on wings like eagles; they will run and not grow weary, they will walk and not be faint (Isa. 40:31).

March 26: **God's Testing**

> *Fine gold is recognized when it is tested.*
> —Leonardo da Vinci

How do we know if we actually have a heart of gold? God tests us. In the same way that gold is put through the fire to rid it of impurities, we can be led into the presence of temptation so we can see what we're actually made of. God isn't the one who tempts us or puts the evil desires in our hearts, but He does allow the temptation to test us. We shouldn't pray to go untested but rather that we would overcome temptation and pass the test. When we do succumb to temptation's tests, ask God to reveal the greed, lust, unforgiveness, and other impurities in our hearts so we may repent, change, and grow more like Christ.

Search me, God, and know my heart; test me and know my anxious thoughts. See if there is any offensive way in me, and lead me in the way everlasting (Ps. 139:23–24).

March 27: Finding Ourselves

Until you have given up your self to Him you will not have a real self.
—C. S. Lewis

We hear of people who go away to college, travel the world, quit their jobs, or leave bad relationships to find themselves because they're feeling lost in life. They say, "New year, new me," and they chop off their hair, get piercings or tattoos, start working out, or begin new relationships. None of these endeavors are wrong, but they aren't true solutions to finding ourselves. Jesus said, "Whoever finds his life will lose it, and whoever loses his life for my sake will find it" (Matt. 10:39 ESV). In other words, if we continue looking to find ourselves in the things of this world, we will be restlessly looking for the rest of our short lives. But if we faithfully lose ourselves to the causes of Jesus, then we will find our true identity in Him, which will last not only in this lifetime but in the next.

For in Christ Jesus you are all sons of God, through faith (Gal. 3:26 ESV).

March 28: **Wounds to Wisdom**

Turn your wounds into wisdom.
—Oprah Winfrey

You know that soldiers have been through something when they have the battle scars to prove it. Soldiers wear their battle scars like a Purple Heart; the battle scars are now as much a part of them as a birthmark. Throughout life, we also fight battles that scar us—so-called friends betray us, we're unemployed unexpectedly, or sickness afflicts us. Although battle scars may always be part of us, eventually God can take away the pain they brought. Ultimately, battle scars can be used to strengthen our faith and resolve. Sooner or later, our faith makes us wiser so we are better able to endure the next battles we face.

He heals the brokenhearted and binds up their wounds (Ps. 147:3 ESV).

March 29: **Say Yes**

Never allow a person to tell you no
who doesn't have the power to say yes
—Eleanor Roosevelt

The answer is yes. "Yes, Lord; yes to Your perfect will because there is no better feeling in the world than being used by You. So, God, if You're going to do anything, don't do it without me. My life is a living sacrifice. I'm Your catalyst. I'm your game-changer. I'm Your servant." Whatever God needs, whenever and wherever He needs it, make your answer yes.

But let your statement be, "Yes, yes" or "No, no"; anything beyond these is of evil (Matt. 5:37 NASB).

March 30: **Sharing without Fear**

The only God-ordained fear is the fear of God, and if we fear Him, we don't have to fear anyone or anything else.
—Mark Batterson

God calls us to share the gospel boldly, clearly, and accurately—leaving nothing out—and without fear of people. What does that actually look like with our unbelieving friends? As we become friends with people, we ought to be up-front with them about our intentions—that we hope they come to a saving faith in Christ and that we will still love them (and want to be friends with them) even if they don't. Then they're not surprised five years later when all of a sudden we express this hope because they knew our intentions all along. Most of us do not live in a region of the world where we have to fear persecution as a result of sharing the gospel, but we do fear losing our friends, which hinders us from sharing. As long as we share the gospel with a healthy fear (or reverence) of a holy God who has given us mercy and grace to save us, we have nothing or nobody to fear. Our motives are pure to fulfill His purpose for us in our very short time on this earth.

We are therefore Christ's ambassadors, as though God were making His appeal through us. We implore you on Christ's behalf: Be reconciled to God (2 Cor. 5:20).

March 31: **Nothing Like God's Grace**

Grace, like water, flows to the lowest part.
—Philip Yancey

Aren't we grateful for a God who pursues us? God is the Good Shepherd who leaves the 99 for the one who is lost. He heals the spiritually blind to give them sight to see Him in all His glory. He takes us from a spiritual death of sin and shame to give us a new life of joy and peace in Him. That is grace. We cannot earn it, we don't deserve it, and there's nothing like it in the entire world. There's nobody so lost that they cannot be found. There's no sin that God's grace cannot cover. There's no life that God's grace cannot alter.

Let us then with confidence draw near to the throne of grace, that we may receive mercy and find grace to help in time of need (Heb. 4:16 ESV).

April 1: **Playing to Win**

If you don't have time to do it right,
when will you have time to do it over?
—John Wooden

In the game of basketball, the coach knows best, and in the game of life, God knows best. You may have played the first quarter of the year without God, but today is the first day of the second quarter. Quit trying to be the star of your own show; hand the show over to the Savior. When God calls the shots—whether it is how you treat people, how you spend your time or money, what you allow to consume your thoughts or attention—you always win.

Put to death therefore what is earthly in you: sexual immorality, impurity, passion, evil desire, and covetousness, which is idolatry (Col. 3:5 ESV).

April 2: **Law or Grace?**

Faith is the key that opens the door of grace.
—Rafael Cruz

Evaluate yourself honestly. Is your faith in Jesus centered on what you do for Him or on what Jesus did on the cross? If Christianity is a bunch of do's and don'ts—law—then that makes it the same as any other major world religion. However, accepting the love God freely gave you—grace—causes you to live by faith in Jesus. You obey Jesus because you love Him for what He did for you on the cross. Those stuck in a law-centered religion cannot understand this love-love relationship.

For the law was given by Moses, but grace and truth came by Jesus Christ (John 1:17 KJV).

April 3: Befriending

I don't like that man. I must get to know him better.
—Abraham Lincoln

Love your neighbor as thyself. Sure, God, loves everyone. But some people are just so hard to like! What if we took the approach to people that many of us took to eating our vegetables when we were toddlers? The broccoli looks gross and has a putrid stench, but it's on our plate, and we have to eat it. Some people are in our lives for a reason. Once we decide to deal with them—like eating broccoli—it proves to be a healthy choice. We may even make a lot of new friends.

And as you wish that others would do to you, do so to them (Luke 6:31 ESV).

April 4: An Uncompromising Christian Example

Remember who you are. Don't compromise for anyone, for any reason. You are a child of the Almighty God. Live that truth.
—Lysa TerKeurst

Whenever you are with people who do not know God and do not live a Christian lifestyle, and when they behave and talk in a manner that is displeasing to God, you may wonder what the best way is to conduct yourself. Do you let them know that you disapprove of what they did, or do you stay quiet? What is the best way to stay friends without participating in their sin? These are not easy questions, but you do know for certain that you cannot compromise your character by joining them in their sin. Pray today that you will not give in to temptation and that you will have the discernment to carry yourself in a way that is not judgmental while still being a positive Christian example. That is a tightrope to walk, but empowered by the Holy Spirit, you can be who God has called you to be so others will eventually come to a saving faith in Him.

In everything set them an example by doing what is good. In your teaching show integrity, seriousness and soundness of speech that cannot be condemned, so that those who oppose you may be ashamed because they have nothing bad to say about us (Titus 2:7–8).

April 5: Travel Light

A duffel bag of weariness, a hanging bag of grief. A backpack of doubt, an overnight bag of fear. Lugging luggage is exhausting!
—Max Lucado

When I traveled throughout Israel, I initially put some books in my backpack in case I got bored at some point in the day. For a few hours, it was manageable carrying the backpack around, but I found out very soon that doing it sunup to sundown was a burden. Although I wanted to carry the books, I didn't need to. As soon as I left the books behind, the tension in my back was gone. In much the same way, we carry burdens that we have no business carrying. A bag of grief here and a bag of guilt there, and before long we've carried them for years. If this habit is your tendency, I urge you to leave your burdens behind. Take a load off and travel light.

Give your burdens to the LORD, and he will take care of you. He will not permit the godly to slip and fall (Ps. 55:22 NLT).

April 6: **Fervent Prayers**

Fervent prayers produce phenomenal results.
—Woodrow Kroll

Some of us are fine praying over our food, but it is difficult for us to ask God to move on our behalf. We pray prayers that are small and neglect to pray big prayers. Jesus said, "You can ask for anything in my name, and I will do it, so that the Son can bring glory to the Father" (John 14:13 NLT). If what we are asking for will bring glory to God, we should feel comfortable asking for it. Often God chooses not to answer our prayers on our timeline, and we have to cling to God and trust Him for a breakthrough. In other words, we must exhibit faith, patience, and perseverance. God doesn't always answer our prayers in the exact way we are expecting, but in one way or another, He will come through for me and for you.

Therefore I tell you, whatever you ask for in prayer, believe that you have received it, and it will be yours (Mark 11:24).

April 7: **God-Interrupted Plans**

Where God guides, God provides.
—Chuck Smith

It is often difficult for us to yield to the leading of the Holy Spirit if it means we are to let go of something—maybe a job, a relationship, or a habit—to risk coming away empty-handed. It usually feels easier to settle into our current course than to brave charting waters of the unknown. Deep down, though, we know we can't stay where we are because we won't like the ultimate destination. Worse, it could lead to an even bigger heartbreak or self-sabotage later. We must trust that God truly does have an individual plan for us, and it always revolves around nothing less than His own glory. When we're living in a way that fails to bring Him glory, it's a good indicator that we must make a change. Just as Abraham sacrificially let go of Isaac to show God that He put nothing above Him, we, too, must show God that we are willing to let go of anything to follow His lead. God provided a ram in the thicket for Abraham to sacrifice in Isaac's stead, and God will provide in unique ways that we don't initially foresee when we choose to obey the Spirit's lead. The simple lesson is that we must let go of whatever holds us back to let God have His way.

For the Lord *God is a sun and shield; the* Lord *bestows favor and honor; no good thing does he withhold from those whose walk is blameless* (Ps. 84:11).

April 8: Silent Influence

Nothing is so potent as the silent influence of a good example.
—James Kent

"There is just something different about you," they say. You walk into a room confidently exuding Christ. Maybe it is a warm smile that casts light on a dark soul. Or maybe it's a comforting hug, and they know they are not alone. Perhaps it's a gracious spirit as you walk humbly, never stealing God's glory by allowing a compliment to go to your head. It is a silent influence; nothing else has to be said.

But if Christ is in you, then even though your body is subject to death because of sin, the spirit gives life because of righteousness (Rom. 8:10).

April 9: Believing God in Faith

Faith is trust or commitment to what you think is true.
—William Lane Craig

There comes a point when we've pleaded with God enough for our breakthrough, and we have to believe that God will deliver on His promises as if He's already done so. Jesus told his disciples, "Therefore I tell you, whatever you ask for in prayer, believe that you have received it, and it will be yours"(Mark 11:24). We, also His disciples, must trust that God will still do for us today what He did back then. That requires faith in God beyond what we can physically see. We may not have now what we've asked for from God, but just as Jacob held on to God to receive his blessing, we, too, must hold on to God's promise that He will move on our behalf. Let's reaffirm our faith in God today when we pray.

And Jesus said to him, "If you can'! All things are possible for one who believes" (Mark 9:23 ESV).

April 10: How to Eat an Elephant

Begin with the end in mind.
—Stephen Covey

Question: How do you swallow an elephant? Answer: One bite at a time. When life has you overburdened and there seems to be no end in sight, remember your overarching mission and allow each of the goals you set to flow from it. For some, that might mean radically reconstructing daily activities to pursue life's purpose. Pray today that God can give you the wisdom to know how to accomplish God's will.

I press on toward the goal for the prize of the upward call of God in Christ Jesus (Phil. 3:14 ESV).

April 11: Changing How We See Ourselves

The eye sees only what the mind is prepared to comprehend.
—Robertson Davies

At times, we might have lost, but that does not make us losers. Losing is an act; it is not who we are. Sickness is not a natural state; it is a current condition. We must see ourselves as healthy people in need of healing. We may have been victimized, but we do not have to live the rest of our lives as victims; we can be victors in the name of Jesus. Changing how we understand ourselves is fundamental to building our faith and seeing God do miracles in our lives.

Now thanks be to God who always leads us in triumph in Christ (2 Cor. 2:14 NKJV).

April 12: **Strangely Wrapped Packages**

That's not a knife . . . that's a knife.
—Michael J. "Crocodile" Dundee

One Christmas, I asked for a Swiss Army knife. I was eight years old, and there was no sweet-talkin' my mother. Her answer was no. I knew I'd have to petition my father. Surely he could understand a boy's desire for a knife. It came time to open presents. I'd opened every single one, but no knife. My father said, "Wait a minute." He went to his room and brought back a package larger than I, and I thought to myself, "I asked for a knife, not a bicycle!" He handed it to me, and the package felt oddly light. I ripped off the wrapping paper and opened the cardboard box only to find that there was yet another box inside, then another, another, and another. Although this was incredibly annoying, I began to smile. I just knew my knife was inside. It took me about eight minutes to get to the last box that had the Swiss logo printed on it. I opened it, and there it was: a red Swiss Army knife with every tool a boy could ever need. Likewise, God is all about giving good gifts to His children. However, sometimes His best gifts come in strangely wrapped packages.

If you, then, though you are evil, know how to give good gifts to your children, how much more will your Father in heaven give good gifts to those who ask him! (Matt. 7:11).

April 13: **Hooked**

A bad day of fishing is better than a good day at work.

—Unknown

As a young child, I went on a fishing trip to Iceland with my family. My mother, who was an eager novice fisherman, connected a three-pronged hook with feathers to her line and cast it into a blue horizon. But unfortunately for her, she caught her rear-end instead. Our family laughed together all the way to the emergency room. Like the fishermen who became Jesus's disciples, we as followers of Christ are to become "fishers of men" who reel people in to the kingdom of God. Let's pray today that God will give us the courage to share the good news and to become fishers of people.

"Come, follow me," Jesus said, "and I will send you out to fish for people" (Matt. 4:19).

April 14: **Different Views**

We view things not only from different sides, but with different eyes.

—Blaise Pascal

Picture yourself with faithful followers, everyone with different views of Jesus as He hangs on the cross. Their views depend on where they are standing in the spectrum of Mount Calvary. They are all looking at the same Christ, but some see His face, while others see His back with the stripes that will bring healing. Still today, people have different views of the Savior according to their needs. That should give us love for one another, realizing that although they may not see Him like we do because of denominational differences, we're all looking at the same Christ.

And my God will meet all your needs according to the riches of his glory in Christ Jesus (Phil. 4:19).

April 15: **God Loves You in Spite of You**

A friend is one who knows you and loves you just the same.
—Elbert Hubbard

David said, "You know what your servant is really like, Sovereign LORD" (2 Sam. 7:20 NLT). God knows everything about you, even the sides you don't show anyone else—your biggest flaws, deepest fears, and the people you struggle to forgive. David, known as a man after God's own heart, also stated, "Thank you for making me so wonderfully complex! Your workmanship is marvelous—how well I know it" (Ps. 139:14 NLT). God intricately created every part of you so you can willfully choose to fellowship and commune with Him. He loves you unconditionally and is the best friend you can ever have!

I praise you because I am fearfully and wonderfully made; your works are wonderful, I know that full well (Ps. 139:14).

April 16: **Christ in You**

Great and good are seldom the same man.
—Winston Churchill

All religions have morality, but what sets Christianity apart? One word: Jesus. It has to be or life becomes about how good we try to be, forgetting how great God is. Jesus, who was without sin, fully man, and fully God, died and rose again so we can enter a relationship with Him. Jesus lives in the believer. A fresh experience with God enables us to embody His ways. We can never be good enough without Him. Today, let's go throughout our day empowered with knowledge that Jesus lives in the believer.

Examine yourselves to see whether you are in the faith; test yourselves. Do you not realize that Christ Jesus is in you—unless, of course, you fail the test? (2 Cor. 13:5).

April 17: **Waiting for God**

The man who goes alone can start today; but he who travels with another must wait till that other is ready.
—Henry David Thoreau

God gave Joseph a dream, and then his brothers sold him into slavery. It was 13 years before Joseph's dream came to pass. At times, Joseph must have thought, "This is your divine plan, God?" Your dream may not materialize as fast as you'd like, but don't lose hope while you are in the waiting process. Pray today that you will place your faith confidently in Christ who blesses those who consistently choose to follow Him wherever He leads.

Wait for the LORD; Be strong and let your heart take courage; Yes, wait for the LORD (Ps. 27:14 NASB).

April 18: **Garbage in, Garbage Out**

If the devil can get you laughing at someone else's sin or transgressions . . . you will not take your own transgressions that seriously.
—Adrian Rogers

If we read trashy literature and watch trashy movies, our thoughts, words, and eventually our actions will be trashy. Christians shouldn't hide from the world in a cave and avoid pop culture like the plague, but we should still be sensitive to whatever the Holy Spirit prompts us to do when He convicts us of activities we should avoid. Let's pray today that we will have the courage of our convictions to avoid a lifestyle that would grieve the Holy Spirit.

When he [the Holy Spirit] comes, he will prove the world to be in the wrong about sin and righteousness and judgment (John 16:8).

April 19: **Provision for the Vision**

When God gives us a vision, he gives us the provision.
—Jan Greenwood

If God has put a vision in your heart, then trust that He will give the provision to see it come to fruition. His name in Hebrew is Jehovah Jireh, which means the Lord will provide. It's in His character and DNA to provide for those who are His children because He loves us. It takes an element of faith to trust God when setting out to fulfill a vision He has given you for your life. It takes faith when the bank account is getting low or there are adversaries opposing you. Continue to pray daily that you will continue to trust Him, because God is a good God who will always provide in one way or another.

For the LORD God is a sun and shield; the LORD bestows favor and honor. No good thing does he withhold from those who walk uprightly (Ps. 84:11 ESV).

April 20: **Handling Our Haters**

It is not the critic who counts . . . The credit belongs to the man who is actually in the arena.
—Theodore Roosevelt

People who are movers and shakers gain a lot of friends and followers, but they also draw critics and haters. Anytime we seek to do something new that's different from the status quo, we should expect opposition from our haters. The opposite is probably also true in that if we don't have haters, then we aren't making too much of a difference. This isn't an excuse to eagerly look for conflict and strife with others—we must always "Do all that [we] can to live in peace with everyone" (Rom. 12:8 NLT)—but naturally there will be people who don't like us or like what we're about no matter what we do or say. So, we must decide to let our haters keep on hating, choosing to ignore them, so that we can focus on moving and shaking in the arena God has called us to. Then we can become all God has called us to be.

If the world hates you, know that it has hated me before it hated you (John 15:18 ESV).

April 21: Purpose in the Pain

Experience is not what happens to you. It is what you do with what happens to you. Don't waste your pain; use it to help others.
—Rick Warren

God can use our most painful experiences to help others who are going through similar circumstances. The pain is not in vain. The most complete form of healing is when we are able to turn our misery into our ministry. May we not just pray that God would heal us so we can carry on as normal (and normalcy may not be possible, depending on what brought about the pain). Rather, pray that He would heal us so we can use whatever we have gone through to comfort others and reveal the love of Jesus to a hurting world so they can place their hope in a God who heals and saves.

He comforts us in all our troubles so that we can comfort others. When they are troubled, we will be able to give them the same comfort God has given us (2 Cor. 1:4 NLT).

April 22: A Bath of Praise

Wash your face every morning in a bath of praise.
—Charles Spurgeon

Just as we wash away rheum (sleepy) from our eyes that hinders us from seeing clearly in the morning, we have to wash away whatever hinders the eyes of our hearts from seeing clearly. God knows that our default settings can tend to think the worst in others. He knows we can get hung up on the guilt of the past and be less than grateful for what we have. We begin to see clearly when we praise God simply for who He is and not just for what He can do for us. God is Jesus Christ, the King of kings and Lord of lords who loved us enough to lower Himself to the cross to die for our sins and the sins of the world so we could be saved. If God never did anything else for us, He's already done more than enough. We simply praise God because He is worthy. This little tweak in how we pray can greatly alter our day by affecting how we see and understand God.

Let us praise God for his glorious grace, for the free gift he gave us in his dear Son! (Eph. 1:6 GNT).

April 23: **Keeping the Peace**

First keep the peace within yourself,
then you can also bring peace to others.
—Thomas à Kempis

Living out WWJD (What would Jesus do?) is sometimes easier said than done when we are ridiculed, mocked, or abused by competitive coworkers or belligerent bosses. It's not easy when angry drivers cut us off or flick us off in traffic, or when people who don't know anything about us or our situations troll us on social media. No matter what they say or do, work with all of your heart to keep the peace, both within yourself and in every one of your relationships. It may not be easy to try to live this way, but we will be more fulfilled if we do.

Do not repay evil with evil or insult with insult. On the contrary, repay evil with blessing, because to this you were called so that you may inherit a blessing (1 Pet. 3:9).

April 24: Ain't Seen Nothin' Yet

You ain't seen nothin' yet.

—Randy Bachman

Jesus was nowhere near Nathanael and therefore shouldn't have physically been able to see him. But Nathanael was astonished that Jesus saw him and knew his name without ever meeting him. He exclaimed, "Rabbi, you are the Son of God; you are the king of Israel" (John 1:49). Jesus responded, "You believe because I told you I saw you under the fig tree. You will see greater things than that" (John 1:50). The lessons for Nathanael are also true for us: (1) we have a God who is omniscient and knows us intimately whether we choose to get to know Him or not, (2) we have not begun to touch the surface of all an omnipotent God wants to do in and through our lives. We ain't seen nothin' yet. Today, let's pray that we will seek to know God so He can begin to do the miraculous in our lives.

Ah, Lord GOD! It is you who have made the heavens and the earth by your great power and by your outstretched arm! Nothing is too hard for you (Jer. 32:17 ESV).

April 25: The Joy of the Lord

Joy is strength.

—Mother Teresa

When we lack joy for whatever reason, we must turn our eyes to God and allow Him to be our source. This is a very different kind of joy than the momentary happiness of having everything go our way. Instead, it is a deep abiding joy in God that is bigger than all our circumstances. The people of Israel experienced the grief of being exiled from their homeland, and many of them lost their loved ones forever. Once they returned home, Nehemiah told them, "Go and enjoy choice food and sweet drinks. . . . Do not grieve, for the joy of the LORD is your strength" (Neh. 8:10). This isn't to say they never felt grief again, but they were encouraged to find their joy in God. The action item Nehemiah tasked them and us with is to "enjoy." In other words, sometimes we have to rejoice anyway and trust that God will fill us with His joy and be our strength, even amid sorrow and grief.

Rejoice in the Lord always. I will say it again: Rejoice! (Phil. 4:4).

April 26: The Stench of Sin

> *You stink.*
> —Maverick (*Top Gun*)

Thirty of us were in a semi-circle seated on the floor around Mrs. Green as she read a story to our class. My third-grade tummy ached, and everything in me wanted to hold it. No! Go! Abruptly she asked, "Who did that?" Humiliated, my little hand went up. She sprayed me with Lysol and ordered me to use the restroom. That day, I learned that farting was social suicide. Sometimes, people use and abuse God's grace by spraying on a little spiritual Lysol to take away the stench of their sin. However, they go on committing the same sins, and ultimately, their hearts still stink. When God's love truly takes hold of our hearts, we are radically transformed and learn that because we love Him, we also want to live for Him.

> *Dead flies make a perfumer's oil stink, so a little foolishness is weightier than wisdom and honor* (Eccles. 10:1 NASB).

April 27: Petition and Praise

> *For every man, good and bad, is bound to praise God,*
> *and to be thankful for all that he hath received,*
> *and to do it as well as he can, rather than leave it undone.*
> —John Piper

Our prayers sometimes go a little like this: "Dear God, I know we don't talk as much I'd like. Things have been crazy, but I just wanted to let You know I was thinking about You." Then the good part: "I really am going to try to behave better. And oh, by the way, You do know I applied for that job, right? Before wrapping up, I have to go, but be sure to bless me when you get the chance. Love ya! Amen." When Paul and Silas were locked up in prison (Acts 16), they never petitioned God to get them out. Instead, they praised Him. God is omniscient, so He already knew what they needed. And He most assuredly knows our needs for today. Just as God sent an earthquake to set Paul and Silas free, He will also provide for our needs. May our prayers become more praise-focused than petition-focused so we will glorify God simply because He is worthy of our praise.

I will extol you, my God and King, and bless your name forever and ever (Ps. 145:1 ESV).

April 28: Good Habits

Good habits, once established are just as hard to break as are bad habits.
—Robert Puller

To quit bad habits, replace them with good habits. Instead of starting the day stressed by turning on the news, start the day in prayer and in the Word. Instead of spending money on unhealthy fast food, save money by meal prepping healthier foods. We can end the day engrossed in emails only to have a hard time falling asleep, or we can lull ourselves to sleep by reading an enjoyable book. Each day, we make choices that determine how our days will go. Let's pray that God will give us wisdom to make good choices so we can live our best lives.

Keep vigilant watch over your heart; that's where life starts (Prov. 4:23 MSG).

April 29: **Opportunity in Adversity**

*Comfort and prosperity have never enriched the world
as much as adversity has.*
—Billy Graham

Adversity can be exactly what we need in order to grow. We may never dig deeper within ourselves to explore new ideas, opportunities, or relationships unless the status quo is stagnating us or we simply do not have any other choice but to make a change. A mother bird will move further away from the nest to beckon her baby bird forward, or she will even push the bird out of the nest so it spreads its wings to fly. In the same way, God sometimes moves ahead of us to call us to follow Him. He even allows uncomfortable circumstances to prick us a little so we step out of our comfort zones to gain new ground. Accepting change and taking risks can be extremely difficult. But just as the mother bird knows the baby will die in the nest if it doesn't eventually leave, the consequences of inaction can often be much worse for us than taking leaps of faith. Sometimes, the adversity we face is just that and not anything more, but other times, God has a message in the midst of it. May we draw closer to God to hear His still small voice so we can discern the difference.

So faith comes from hearing, and hearing through the word of Christ (Rom. 10:17 ESV).

April 30: **Enjoyment vs. Achievement**

People rarely succeed unless they have fun in what they are doing.
—Dale Carnegie

If we measure success solely by achievement, we might find that we are constantly under pressure to meet demands we place on ourselves or others place on us. When we achieve, we are happy for a short period of time before we set another goal. And thus our lives can feel like rat races. When we fail to achieve, we may feel as if all our efforts were for nothing, and we are sorely disappointed. If we measure success by enjoyment, however, then we decipher whether we are truly happy achieving our objectives. Granted, some ventures are not meant to be fun but rather necessary and difficult in the short term so we can enjoy life in the long term. In general, we must strive to enjoy our journey along the way to reach our destination because that is what will make a life well-lived.

So I concluded there is nothing better than to be happy and enjoy ourselves as long as we can. And people should eat and drink and enjoy the fruits of their labor, for these are gifts from God (Eccles. 3:12–13 NLT).

May 1: Only God Can Fulfill

We pursue God because, and only because, He has first put an urge within us that spurs us to the pursuit.
—A. W. Tozer

There exists a gaping hole in our hearts that we hope to fill. We pursue possessions and positions and think prestige and popularity will bring happiness. But none of that fulfills us. God created us this way so the only One who is gargantuan and glorious enough to fill the hole and make our hearts whole is God. Life will always feel empty without Him. Let us pray today that we will be committed to the belief that there is no substitute for knowing and being known by Christ and that we may help as many people as possible come to do the same.

Let him not trust in emptiness, deceiving himself; for emptiness will be his reward (Job 15:31 NASB).

May 2: **Preparation and God's Providence**

I will study and prepare myself, and someday my chance will come.
—Abraham Lincoln

We often characterize the account of David and Goliath as an underdog story. We look at David as though he were somehow lucky or actually a better fighter than Goliath. And that overlooks the real moral of the story. Actually, the God of Israel orchestrated every event in David's life that would lead him to the moment when he would face Goliath. God had allowed David to first face a lion and then a bear to hone his slingshot ability. God had David's father send him to the battlefield to give his brothers food, and God stirred King Saul's heart to allow David to fight this battle. Yes, David had prepared for the fight by becoming an expert slinger, but it was only by God's providence that the fight ever happened. That's because it is God who controls the course of world events and tears down and sets up kings (Dan. 2:21). David could never have calculated the sequence of events that made him instantly famous and eventually king of Israel. It was always God in his providence. Here's the lesson for us. We can do everything in our own power to set ourselves up for success, but ultimately, the victory belongs to God. Just as God orchestrated the events in David's life, He orchestrates the events in ours. Today, let's pray that we will be people who are prepared for the day of battle. But let's also pray that we won't hesitate to give God all the glory due Him for the victory.

The horse is prepared for the day of battle, but the victory belongs to the LORD (Prov. 21:31 NLT).

May 3: Childlike Imagination

You can't depend on your eyes when your imagination is out of focus.
—Mark Twain

When I was six years old, I loved Legos. One reason was because I created what I saw in my mind. I used my imagination, and anything was possible. After a few hours of hard play, I brought my vision to fruition, and voilà, I had a medieval castle. The problem with many adults is not that they lose their imagination but that they allow life experiences to limit it. A few failed attempts and we say, "I can't" or "This will never work." Before you can ever innovate, you have to first let go of inhibition so you can begin to fully imagine all the possibilities. Today, prayerfully ask God to open the eyes of your heart so you see all the possibilities.

With God all things are possible (Matt. 19:26 NKJV).

May 4: Remaining Faithful in Suffering

The same everlasting Father who cares for you today will take care of you tomorrow and every day. Either He will shield you from suffering, or He will give you unfailing strength to bear it.
—St. Francis de Sales

Often, we go through circumstances in life that challenge our faith in God. Perhaps it is an unexpected layoff or a business deal that did not go through. Maybe it's people we thought we could trust who proved untrustworthy, or maybe a child gets in trouble or a spouse gets sick. Naturally, these circumstances can feel crushing, but we cannot lose our hope in a God who is firmly in control. We must trust that God will keep His word to always work all things for the good and to give us peace that will surpass all understanding. We must commit that even if God does not turn our circumstances around on our timelines—or at all, for that matter—our faith in Him will never be contingent on what He does for us but on who He is. Let us pray today that we will have unshakable faith so that in everything, even in suffering, Christ is glorified because we remain faithful. And let us pray that others will come to know Him by watching how we respond to suffering.

You will keep in perfect peace those whose minds are steadfast, because they trust in you (Isa. 26:3).

May 5: Protected Steps

The greatest mistake we make is living in constant fear that we will make one.
—John C. Maxwell

Have you ever felt that making life decisions is like evading landmines that were set to detonate at the first erroneous step? Some forgo the peace of mind God desires for them because they dread the mistakes of the past or worry about failing again in the future. The fear of failure only hinders us from taking chances and moving forward. When we are walking with our heavenly Father, we must have faith that He will protect and provide for us as He directs our paths. Let's pray today that we will trust Him every step of the way.

The LORD makes firm the steps of the one who delights in him; though he may stumble, he will not fall, for the LORD upholds him with his hand (Ps. 37:23–24).

May 6: **Rejoicing in Today**

Yesterday is gone. Tomorrow has not yet come.
We have only today. Let us begin.
—Mother Teresa

Regret and worry are useless emotions because they neither change the past nor help us in the future. They only hinder us from enjoying the present. God wants us fully engaged today. We must not miss opportunities to be a light to others because our minds are clouded with despair. Let us reflect on how God has provided for us in the past so we will trust that He is working out all things for our good to give us a hope and a future even when it does not feel like it. And may we be a force for God's goodness to others in the present. By doing this, we may not change our circumstances right away or ever, but God begins to change our hearts to be molded more in His likeness. In spite of the setbacks and disappointments of life, the mark of a Christian is that we persist to become more like Jesus.

This is the day that the LORD has made; let us rejoice and be glad in it (Ps. 118:24 ESV).

May 7: **Nation under God**

And without God, democracy will not and cannot long endure.
If we ever forget that we're one nation under God,
then we will be a nation gone under.
—Ronald Reagan

Even after God renamed Jacob "Israel," for years he still went by Jacob. After his name change, tragedy struck his daughter, his sons sinned, idolatry was rampant in his camp, and life wore him down, so he needed reminding. God told Jacob to go back to Bethel (the land God had already given him) to dwell there, purify himself, and build an altar (Gen. 35). There, God reminded Jacob of who he was—not Jacob, but Israel, a man from whom a great nation would come. Throughout scripture, Jacob's descendants who formed the nation of Israel also forgot who they were, and God would humble them as a reminder. The lesson for Israel is also true for us as individuals and for us as a nation. We must not forget who we are under God. Whenever we do, we must go back to the places we first experienced Him. Let us humble ourselves to get our hearts right with God, keep Him first, and pray that He will bless us and bless our nation.

If my people, who are called by my name, will humble themselves, and pray and seek my face and turn from their wicked ways, then I will hear from heaven, and I will forgive their sin and will heal their land (2 Chron. 7:14).

May 8: Giving God Everything

You can't really give God tomorrow; you can only give him what you have, and today is all you have.
—Tim LaHaye

If God asked you to return everything He's ever given you—the relationships with your spouse and children, your dearest friendships, your health, your earthly possessions, your hopes and dreams—would you still serve Him? God would never ask because your stuff actually already belongs to Him (Ps. 24:1). What God wants is your heart. Take the time today to offer your life back to the giver of everything so your heart is right with Him.

Therefore, I urge you, brothers and sisters, in view of God's mercy, to offer your bodies as a living sacrifice, holy and pleasing to God—this is your true and proper worship (Rom. 12:1).

May 9: **God Cares**

God is attracted to weakness. He can't resist those who humbly and honestly admit how desperately they need him.
—Jim Cymbala

You may think that El Shaddai who created the universe, holds every star in place, keeps earth's orbit around the sun, and has a population of 7 billion people to reign over has bigger fish to fry than our measly problems. But that is not true. Our Maker intimately loves His creation so much that He has counted every hair on your head. Call on God in your time of need, believing He has all the power to help.

This is the confidence we have in approaching God: that if we ask anything according to his will, he hears us. And if we know that he hears us—whatever we ask—we know that we have what we asked of him (1 John 5:14–15).

May 10: **Rooting Out Weeds**

Whatever is begun in anger ends in shame.
—Benjamin Franklin

My mother, Mimi, has a garden in her backyard where she has faithfully grown fruits and vegetables. Constantly, she grooms the garden, rooting out weeds. Anger, bitterness, and unforgiveness are weeds in your spiritual garden. If you harbor those spiritual weeds in your heart, even for a short period of time, they hinder the growth of life-giving plants such as love, joy, and peace. Eventually, weeds multiply and overtake a garden. We must root out the weeds of anger, bitterness, and unforgiveness in our lives by submitting to the power of the Holy Spirit. One day, my mother proudly gave me a fresh cucumber; her harvest blessed me as it has others. Each day, you must groom your spiritual garden with prayer and God's Word. Eventually, your garden will not only bless you but also others.

But the fruit of the Spirit is love, joy, peace, forbearance, kindness, goodness, faithfulness, gentleness and self-control. (Gal. 5:22–23).

May 11: **Words**

Words which do not give the light of Christ increase the darkness.
—Mother Teresa

Jesus told his followers, "Before long, the world will not see me anymore, but you will see me" (John 14:19). Picture your words as a flashlight in a dark world; you either point people to Christ or away from Him. While we may not physically see Him, Christ is Emmanuel, and He is always with us. May we use our words effectively to share the Light of the world to push back the darkness.

No one lights a lamp and hides it in a clay jar or puts it under a bed. Instead, they put it on a stand, so that those who come in can see the light (Luke 8:16).

May 12: **Be Ordinary**

Conformity is the jailer of freedom and the enemy of growth.
—John F. Kennedy

Do you want to be ordinary? Then let your light shine so dimly that people can barely tell you're a Christian. Say the carnal things nonbelievers say, go wherever they go, and do what they do. Think about what's popular instead of what's eternal. Worry more and pray less. Live for earthly pleasures, forgetting about your Maker. Conform to the world and be ordinary.

Do not conform to the pattern of this world, but be transformed by the renewing of your mind. Then you will be able to test and approve what God's will is—his good, pleasing and perfect will (Rom. 12:2).

May 13: **Spiritual Tug of War**

*Success seems to be largely a matter of hanging on after others
have let go.*

—William Feather

As a child, I watched my favorite cartoon about a cat and mouse—Tom and Jerry. In one episode, Tom's bad angel and good angel both bid for his soul. We, too, have a spiritual tug-of-war within us. The question is this: Will you let go and give in to your vices, or will you hold onto God to stand your ground? Occasionally, you may have a moment of weakness, but by God's enduring grace, you will grow stronger. So let's pray that we never stop doing good.

So then, brothers and sisters, stand firm and hold fast to the teachings we passed on to you, whether by word of mouth or by letter (2 Thess. 2:15).

May 14: **Being Thankful**

*If a fellow isn't thankful for what he's got, he isn't likely to be thankful
for what he's going to get.*

—Frank Clark

Most people would admit that they spend a lot more time thinking about what they wish they had than being thankful for what they have. It is God's nature to want to bless His children, but He expects Christians to show Him thanks for what they have. Today, praise and thank God for what He has already given you with the expectation that He will continue to bless you. Regardless of whether God blesses you now or at all, He is worthy of praise simply for who He is and for what Christ did on the cross. If God never did anything else, He has already done more than enough.

And whatsoever ye do in word or deed, do all in the name of the Lord Jesus, giving thanks to God and the Father by him (Col. 3:17 KJV).

May 15: **Winning Our Battles**

Battles are won in the hearts of men.
—Vince Lombardi

There are battles we as believers go through from time to time that beat us down. If you haven't gone through a battle yet on your journey with God, give it time, and you will. Perhaps it's a spiritual battle wrestling with sin and shame or why God would allow something bad to happen to someone good or even doubting whether God exists at all. Maybe your battle is financial or about your health. Maybe so-called friends betrayed you, or your career hasn't gone the way you'd hoped. No matter what battles you feel you've lost, the war isn't over, and God isn't finished writing your story. God specializes in fighting our battles for us because He loves being the hero in our stories to bring Himself glory. God wants to give us the desires of our hearts, and sometimes He has to kick-start dead hearts to make them beat again. We can then begin to envision endless possibilities and dream new dreams. Fully surrender your heart to God and seek His face so He can begin afresh in you.

Do not be afraid of them; the LORD *your God himself will fight for you* (Deut. 3:22).

May 16: **Caring for Others**

In helping others, we help ourselves.
—Woodrow Kroll

A good way to overcome whatever it is we're battling internally is to focus externally on the needs of others. When we stop to notice that there are others dealing with a set of circumstances that are much worse than what we're going through—not to diminish the battles we go through and the importance of self-care to rest and heal—we often find the best remedy is taking care of the needs of others. Take some time to visit the elderly at a retirement home, or volunteer at a local food bank, or go serve at your church. Do something to give back, and by doing so, we will better ourselves by bettering the lives of others.

Whoever is kind to the poor lends to the LORD, and he will reward them for what they have done (Prov. 19:17).

May 17: Negativity Is a Virus

Optimism is the faith that leads to achievement. Nothing can be done without hope and confidence.
—Helen Keller

Software engineers know that to remove a virus from a computer, they have to be willing to wipe the hard drive. Otherwise, the virus will continue to infect and slow down the computer. Likewise, negativity can infect our hearts. When we lack confidence and there seems to be no hope, God must wipe our hearts clean. God reboots our hearts so we run freely by the Holy Spirit, and therein lies a newfound optimism. Today, let's ask God to wipe us clean and reboot us.

Keep thy heart with all diligence; for out of it are the issues of life (Prov. 4:23 KJV).

May 18: Trailblazers

Do not follow where the path may lead. Go instead where there is no path and leave a trail.
—Ralph Waldo Emerson

There are points in our faith journey where we may have to become trailblazers. What we're setting out to do hasn't been done in this form or fashion before, so we must do something completely new. It is a completely different mindset than simply emulating others since it puts us in a position of having to be innovative. Almost anyone can look at what's already been done before and do the exact same thing, but it takes a person of faith to try to do what's not been tried before. Go blaze a trail, and let God guide you every step of the way.

The Lord makes firm the steps of the one who delights in him (Ps. 37:23).

May 19: Working within Limitations

Stop waiting for what you want, and start working with what you've got. Your greatest limitation is God's greatest opportunity.
—Steven Furtick

Most of us tell ourselves that if I had _____, I would _____ (you fill in the blanks.) Realistically, everyone has limitations, and although it's okay to dream, limitations don't go away because we dream. On the contrary, it's when we embrace and work within our limitations that God can take the little we have and do exceedingly more than we could ever imagine.

And the LORD said unto him, What is that in thine hand? (Exod. 4:2 KJV).

May 20: How to Destroy Your Enemies

The best way to destroy an enemy is to make him a friend.
—Abraham Lincoln

Saul of Tarsus persecuted and killed many Christians. He was, without realizing it, an enemy of God. One day as Saul was on his way, a bright light blinded him, and the voice of Christ asked him why he was persecuting Him. At that point, Saul realized who Christ was, and he became His friend. What if God had given up on being friends with Saul? Saul of Tarsus would not have become the Apostle Paul who wrote half of the New Testament. Paul would not have started the first churches that would carry the good news of Christ to the rest of the world. It all came about because God made an enemy into a friend. Who in your life could you never be friends with? Just maybe that's exactly who God is calling you to befriend.

But I say, love your enemies! Pray for those who persecute you! (Matt. 5:44 NLT).

May 21: Winning the Spiritual Long Run

Perseverance is not a long race; it is many short races one after the other.
—Walter Elliot

By 1999, Hicham El Guerrouj of Morocco had not won every race he had ever run, but that year he finished the mile race with a time of 3:43:13 to become the world record holder. Likewise, Christians will lose races with sin in the pursuit of winning over it in the long run. God does not expect Christians to be perfect, but one of the calling cards of a Christian is a general pattern of righteous living and a "hunger and thirst for righteousness" (Matt. 5:6). God's grace will completely cover sin through the blood of Jesus, so we must let grace be a game-changer for us. As Jesus told the prostitute, "Go now and leave your life of sin" (John 8:11). May we respond to the grace we have been freely given with the pursuit of righteous living so we may glorify God with how we run our race.

Therefore, since we are surrounded by such a great cloud of witnesses, let us throw off everything that hinders and the sin that so easily entangles. And let us run with perseverance the race marked out for us, fixing our eyes on Jesus, the pioneer and perfecter of faith (Heb. 12:1–2).

May 22: **Staying in Awe of Jesus**

There is no question that faith is a key element in effective prayer. On one occasion, Jesus could not do many miracles in a certain place because of the unbelief of the people there.
—Greg Laurie

When Jesus began teaching in his hometown, He taught the people as He had in every other place He had been. But these people treated Him as someone commonplace and familiar. They had known Jesus as a little boy, so they were not in awe of Him as so many others had been. Jesus said, "A prophet is not without honor except in his own town" (Mark 6:4). Consequently, Jesus performed no miracles there. The people there didn't recognize that as Jesus entered His ministry at the age of 30 He had been empowered from on high to teach the gospel and perform miracles. Many of those people were probably not bad people, but they nevertheless missed out on God's favor and blessings. Over time, in our relationship with God, we, too, can begin to pray routine and faithless prayers to a God we are treating as commonplace and familiar. The lesson for those people in Jesus's hometown is true for me and for you. If we want to see Jesus do the miraculous in our lives, we must stay in constant awe of an all-powerful God who can do anything.

Everything is possible for one who believes (Mark 9:23).

May 23: **Amateur**

Every artist was first an amateur.
—Ralph Waldo Emerson

Sometimes, the negative side-effect of our desires to reach our goals causes us to be discontent with our current circumstances. Perhaps we compare ourselves to someone further along or to someone who is a professional at what they do, and we look at ourselves and say, "What do I bring to the table?" or "I will never be good enough." Whether we act, sing, dance, paint, draw, write, speak, or perform, remember that it is okay to be an amateur as long as we are doing our personal best to produce art with excellence in order to glorify God. Also, know that on average, it takes 10,000 hours of practice to become an expert in something. So let's keep to the practice of producing art. May we ask God for patience today as we pray to grow into the people He is calling us to be and that He would use our art to impact the lives of others so they, too, would be inspired to produce art that will glorify God.

And whatever you do, whether in word or deed, do it all in the name of the Lord Jesus, giving thanks to God the Father through him (Col. 3:17).

May 24: Exhibiting Christ

You are the only Bible some unbelievers will ever read.
—John MacArthur

It is important to remember that many will not open a Bible, much less attend a Bible study or church service. Their only contact with Christ will come by way of their experiences with Christians. So a good thing for us to ponder is whether we are acting in a manner that best represents Christ. Most of us would say yes, but some would say no. It's not always easy to live out our faith, but the better we get at living in the Spirit, the sooner we will start to exhibit the fruit of the Spirit—love, joy, peace, forbearance, kindness, goodness, faithfulness, gentleness, and self-control. When we exhibit the Spirit, people will be more inclined to want to hear what we have to say about Christ.

Have this attitude in yourselves which was also in Christ Jesus (Phil. 2:5 NASB).

May 25: No Rollover Minutes

How soon "not now" becomes "never."

—Martin Luther

Before my cell phone company offered unlimited data and minutes plans, it used to offer rollover plans so the minutes I didn't use each month could be used the next month. Unfortunately, real time does not work like rollover minutes because you cannot preserve any moment for a more suitable time in the future. If you are someone who says, "I will live for God later after I have my fun," you may not get the chance. Perhaps you keep telling yourself that you will spend more time with your kids, but the hard truth is that they will grow up, and you will not get back this time with them. Maybe you wanted to start a business, get into shape, write a book, go back to school, or run for office. But you pushed your dream off another day and then weeks and months, and soon it has been years. May the prayer of our hearts be "redeeming the time" (Eph. 5:16 KJV) so we will make the most of the very short time we have on this earth.

So teach us to number our days that we may get a heart of wisdom (Ps. 90:12 ESV).

May 26: Feeling the Burn

The first and worst of all frauds is to cheat one's self.
All sin is easy after that.

—Pearl Bailey

In high school, I wanted to grow in strength, so I found the biggest guy in the gym, a Ronnie Coleman look-alike, and asked him to be my weight-lifting partner. When he noticed I was only going through the motions but not feeling the burn, he would scream, "Treat yourself, son; don't cheat yourself." So I slowed down my lift tempo, used a better form, and executed the exercise with excellence. I'm afraid that as Christians we can operate the same way. We go through the motions of reading our Bibles and going to church but without the fire that only comes from the Holy Ghost. Without it, we only cheat ourselves. My prayer is that today we will ask God to fill us with the fire that comes from the Holy Spirit so we can feel the burn.

God is a Spirit: and they that worship him must worship him in spirit and in truth (John 4:24 KJV).

May 27: God's Word Is a Light

Let God's promises shine on your problems.
—Corrie ten Boom

A flashlight helps us see in the darkness, and God's promises help us see in the midst of our problems. Where do we find God's promises? We find them written throughout scripture, which is God's Word. We must commit to reading and memorizing God's Word in order to speak light to the darkness anytime. God desires that we become so well versed in scripture that it becomes second nature for us to apply it to our lives.

Your word is a lamp for my feet, a light on my path (Ps. 119:105).

May 28: Potential and Pain

Your potential in life is equal to the pain you're willing to endure.
—Craig Groeschel

The pain and suffering we go through in life will strengthen us so the next time we go through something similar, it will not be as difficult as the first time. A weight lifter must endure the pain of soreness after lifting, effectively ripping open a muscle so it can heal and begin to grow in size and strength. No pain, no gain. The more resistance weight lifters are met with on the bench press, the stronger they eventually become. My point is that resistance never feels good, but it is necessary in order for us to grow into the people God is calling us to be. While it may hurt for a while, eventually it makes us into stronger people because we are able to endure more resistance later and help those who happen to be going through painful situations we've already worked through. That's how we realize our true potential in Christ.

Not only that, but we rejoice in our sufferings, knowing that suffering produces endurance, and endurance produces character, and character produces hope (Rom. 5:3–4 ESV).

May 29: Winning Words

Good words are worth much and cost little.
—George Herbert

At the age of five, I lived in Norway. I'd always go to my friend Steinar's house to play video games. Steiner was also five, but he was much scrawnier, wore glasses with extra-thick lenses, and had highlighter blond hair. Anytime he'd lose a video game, he'd scream, "F%$# you, video game." I don't think either of us really understood that the F-word was a bad word; at least I sure didn't. One day, I went out on a boat to fish with my dad—a minister—and some of his friends. We had a fish hooked on the line, but he got away. So naturally, I yelled, "F#@$ you, fish!" My dad just about had a heart attack on that boat, and I learned a valuable lesson that day. Words are contagious because eventually we become like the people we consistently spend time with. If you are spending time with people who speak positive words filled with hope, faith, love, and encouragement, then guess what you'll have to say? Otherwise, you'll probably end up sounding a lot like I did.

Let no corrupting talk come out of your mouths, but only such as is good for building up (Eph. 4:29 ESV).

May 30: **Not Alone**

You are never left alone when you are alone with God.
—Woodrow Kroll

Jesus lived among his disciples for three years of his ministry, fellowshipping and sharing meals, as well as traveling from town to town sharing the gospel. The disciples had become very comfortable having Jesus right there with them. When Jesus would soon ascend to heaven, His disciples felt as if they were losing their friend, Lord, and Savior forever. He assured them that they were not being abandoned as orphans because He would send the Holy Spirit, a comforter who would abide in them. As believers, we sometimes feel all alone because life can be lonely, but we must remember that the Holy Spirit is living in us, to always be with us, comfort us, and guide us. We are never alone.

Turn to me and be gracious to me, for I am lonely and afflicted (Ps. 25:16).

May 31: **Listen First**

Courage is what it takes to stand up and speak.
Courage is also what it takes to sit down and listen.
—Winston Churchill

The saying goes, "God gave you two ears and one mouth because you're supposed to listen twice as much as you talk." To have the opportunities to courageously stand up for truth, sometimes you must courageously listen to the other side first. Learn about their beliefs to effectively engage them. More than likely, they will then reciprocate and pay attention when it is your time to talk.

Let the wise listen and add to their learning, and let the discerning get guidance (Prov. 1:5).

June 1: **Loving without Agendas**

Loving people means caring without an agenda.
As soon as we have an agenda, it's not love anymore.
—Bob Goff

Almost everyone on most days has agendas, whether spoken or unspoken. It's not always wrong to have agendas, but at times they can get in the way of loving other people. I have learned that instead of going up to others to share what I'm offering, I strive to learn what I can about them and how I can help. Maybe there is something I can give—a helping hand, a warm smile, a listening ear, a connection to someone or something, an encouraging word—so they sense the love of God in me. More often than not, if we take care of the needs of others, regardless of whether they ever take an interest in us or our agendas, God, in one way or another, will take care of our needs. The love we give always comes back to us.

Let all that you do be done in love (1 Cor. 16:14 ESV).

June 2: **Call It Like It Is**

To accomplish great things, we must dream as well as act.
—Anatole France

God appeared to Jacob in a dream to let him know that the land he was lying on would be given to him and his descendants. He awoke and named the land Bethel, which means "House of God." Even though the land was still technically known as Luz, Jacob called it like he saw it. Maybe your reality and the dream God has put in your heart don't exactly match yet, but you, too, must call it like you see it. Professing the dream God has put in your heart is the first step of acting in agreement.

He called the name of that place Bethel, but the name of the city was Luz at the first (Gen. 28:19 ESV).

June 3: **Helping and Achieving**

If you can dream it, then you can achieve it. You will get all you want in life if you help enough other people get what they want.
—Zig Ziglar

We cannot reach the God-given dreams He has put in our hearts without soliciting the help of other people. The problem is, too many people have a scarcity mentality. They feel like they have to step on as many people as possible to climb the proverbial ladder in fear that someone will surpass them if they don't. Actually, they'd climb a lot higher in life if they pulled other people up with them as they climbed. God's favor always flows through other people. It's the biblical principle of sowing and reaping. When we give of ourselves to other people, then in one way or another, it is returned to us, and sometimes with dividends.

Give, and it will be given to you. A good measure, pressed down, shaken together and running over, will be poured into your lap. For with the measure you use, it will be measured to you (Luke 6:38).

June 4: **The Fruit of Salvation**

Salvation is not verified by a past act, but by present fruitfulness.
—John MacArthur

What is the fruit of our salvation? It's not a matter of having said a prayer once or having gone through any formal confirmation process. Rather, Jesus said, "By their fruit you will recognize them" (Matt. 7:16). Any tree that isn't producing the fruit of salvation—a desire to live righteously in opposition to sin, to spend time in prayer and God's Word, and to give generously and share the gospel with others—could very well be dead. There are, of course, times as Christians that we fall short or become consumed with life's trials. My point isn't to chastise or cause anyone to question their salvation but rather to encourage us to live so the fruits of our service are clearly visible.

May you always be filled with the fruit of your salvation—the righteous character produced in your life by Jesus Christ—for this will bring much glory and praise to God (Phil. 1:11 NLT).

June 5: Sticks and Stones

Good words are worth much, and cost little.
—George Herbert

"Sticks and stones may break my bones, but words can never hurt me." Is that not the stupidest thing you've ever heard? Words can hurt and often do. The Bible says to "guard your heart" (Prov. 4:23), especially from toxic words and sometimes from toxic people. You may never entirely escape your critics, but your inner circle of friends must be people who speak life and not death (Prov. 18:21) to your dreams, goals, and future. Build the habit of speaking life to your own circumstances as well as to others. Too often, people say whatever pops in their heads, usually negative. Instead, if we have something good to say, let's say it. Always. Strive to be someone people cannot get enough of so people always leave feeling better about themselves after talking with you.

Gracious words are like a honeycomb, sweetness to the soul and health to the body (Prov. 16:24 ESV).

June 6: **Oh, My Bad, Bro**

> *The world forgetting, by the world forgot.*
> —Alexander Pope

Have you ever seen the "Want to get away?" Southwest Airlines commercials? I hung out once with a guy who was the epitome of cool (all the ladies loved Wade). A few ladies said hello to us, and I proceeded to introduce him: "This is my buddy, Graham." Fail. I got Wade's name wrong for what seemed to be 10 of the longest seconds ever. "Oh, my bad, bro." Graham was the guy I'd evidently spent too much time doing ministry with, but Wade didn't know that. I felt like taking the first flight to Bermuda, and I think Wade would have been happy to see me leave. This embarrassing illustration leads me to my biblical tie-in. In the world today, people are usually unashamed to talk about "god," but god is a vague word, especially if and when there are multiple definitions. At any mention of Jesus, their countenance may change because, to some, Jesus is offensive. Never forget the name that is above all names. He is the King of kings and the Lord of lords. He is God all by Himself. His name is Jesus.

Christ is the visible image of the invisible God. He existed before anything was created and is supreme over all creation (Col. 1:15 NLT).

June 7: **Connecting the Dots**

> *You can't connect the dots looking forward; you can only connect them looking backwards. So you have to trust that the dots will somehow connect in your future.*
> —Steve Jobs

Do you remember when you were a kid and played Connect the Dots? The dots formed a picture of a dog, but you didn't know that until you finished connecting the dots. God works out events in our lives in the same way. We go from point A to point B, and we don't see the big picture God is creating yet. When we go from B to K, we may finally start to see what God is creating. We didn't see the big picture amid the pain; we're only able to see the big picture in hindsight after seeing what God did next. All the events in our lives, good or bad, work together for the good. It's only when we truly have this realization about our past that we start to trust God with our future. In the end, we will see God has created a magnificent picture.

And we know that God causes everything to work together for the good of those who love God and are called according to his purpose for them (Rom. 8:28 NLT).

June 8: Christian Cruise Control

You never know God is all you need until God is all you have.
—Rick Warren

On life's journey, sometimes I subconsciously shift gears to drive in Christian cruise control. The shift is subtle, but maybe you've noticed it. Bible reading feels routine, prayer a ritual, church ceremonial, and a cross becomes neck jewelry. Life isn't bad; it's just boring. Ordinary. There's no passion. It was in those times that I first began to live for God and realized how much I desperately needed Christ. I prayed continuously because I depended on God for strength. I read God's Word because I wanted to know Him intimately. In church, I experienced the presence of God. A cross symbolized God's love for me. The fact is that we cannot do Christianity without Christ. Let's retake the wheel to be intentional about following Christ, because when we do, there is no limit to how far we can go.

Patient endurance is what you need now, so that you will continue to do God's will. Then you will receive all that he has promised (Heb. 10:36 NLT).

June 9: Overcoming Fear of Uncertainty

Courage is resistance to fear, mastery of fear, not absence of fear.
—Mark Twain

What would happen if we asked God to remove uncertainties in life so we could live without fear of an unknown future? That would be like thinking we will never be sore again if we all of a sudden quit working out. Sure, we might not be sore again, but we will not grow stronger, either. The best way to overcome soreness is to push through it whenever we continue working out. Likewise, the best way for God to help us is actually not by removing uncertainty. He must keep us in the midst of it, so we will eventually gain perspective to see through it. Let us pray today that we place our trust firmly in God today amid the uncertainties of life.

When I am afraid, I will put my trust in You (Ps. 56:3 NASB).

June 10: Make Small Opportunities Great

Don't wait for extraordinary opportunities.
Seize common occasions and make them great.
—Orison Swett Marden

We often pray to God for a future great opportunity as if whatever opportunities we have now are nowhere near as important. We hope that capitalizing on great opportunities will bring the desired outcomes in our lives. What if God wants us to make the most of the small opportunities that we already have? Maybe we should not wait for God to give us great opportunities but instead simply make the most of our current opportunities. Whether it's our present job, our ample resources, or the family we were blessed to be born into, there are opportunities for greatness every day if we simply take time to notice and capitalize on them. Let us prayerfully go to God today and ask Him to help us make the most of every opportunity, even the small ones.

The master said, "Well done, my good and faithful servant. You have been faithful in handling this small amount, so now I will give you many more responsibilities. Let's celebrate together!" (Matt. 25:23 NLT).

June 11: Don't Stop Shooting

Some people want it to happen, some wish it would happen, others make it happen.
—Michael Jordan

Who told you that you can't? Maybe you've written off the vision God has given you to just wishful thinking. Your biggest critic is you! I have learned that the fear of failure can be worse than the act of failing. In fear, you're pessimistic and paralyzed, but in faith, you're positive and proactive. Don't get me wrong, you do need to map out the X's and the O's to know what you're playing against, but if you've stopped shooting, then get your mind back in the game. Fear puts you on the sidelines; faith gives you the ball to take the shot.

Now faith is the assurance of things hoped for, the conviction of things not seen (Heb. 11:1 ESV).

June 12: Destiny Pushers

Friendship is not something you learn in school. But if you haven't learned the meaning of friendship, you really haven't learned anything.
—Muhammad Ali

Have you ever spent an entire day with a friend and picked up some of their habits? Maybe you subconsciously began to mimic the way they talked, laughed, or joked. If you hang out with people who are angry, who gossip, and are negative, it influences you. It affects not only your sense of peace now but also the level of success you have later. Obviously, you can't avoid some people in life (coworkers, family), but you can choose a close circle of friends who push you to be better. These so-called destiny pushers who speak love, hope, and faith into your life are a catalyst to help you arrive at the future God has for you.

Walk with the wise and become wise, for a companion of fools suffers harm (Prov. 13:20).

June 13: Rerouted

I've always found that anything worth achieving will always have obstacles in the way and you've got to have that drive and determination to overcome those obstacles on route to whatever it is that you want to accomplish.
—Chuck Norris

One day I arrived in Charlotte, but due to a flight delay, I learned I would miss my connecting flight to Houston. "Now what?" I wondered. The airline informed me I would have no choice but to stay overnight in a hotel. I thought, "Oh, great, now I'm stuck in some hole in the wall." To my surprise, they put me in a 4.5-star hotel, a three-room suite. Needless to say, I enjoyed myself. In life, we map out our route, whether it's where we want to attend college, who we date in hopes that we will marry, and whatever field we would like to work in. But we become discouraged when our circumstances do not turn out as we planned. When God reroutes us, let's trust in Him and stay encouraged! Eventually, we will find out that God knew what He was doing all along.

We can make our plans, but the LORD determines our steps (Prov. 16:9 NLT).

June 14: **A God of Miracles**

Your potential is the sum of all the possibilities God has for your life.
—Charles Stanley

Before Jesus ascended to heaven, He told His disciples that those who believe in Him will do even greater works than He did (John 14:12). It seems counterintuitive to think that we as believers can do greater things than Jesus, but through the power of the Holy Spirit, we are equipped with all the power and authority of heaven. It's not us doing anything but God in us, and that changes us and equips us to be catalysts for change in the world. God can use us to heal the sick and perform miracles each day, which ultimately helps illuminate Him to the lost. God is still the same God today that He has always been—a God of miracles. If we yield ourselves fully to the power of the Holy Spirit, then God can use us in ways we never would have thought possible.

God also testified to it by signs, wonders and various miracles, and by gifts of the Holy Spirit distributed according to his will (Heb. 2:4).

June 15: **Not Perfect, and That's Okay**

I try to be as real and honest about everything and very genuine with people and say, "Listen, I'm a Christian, and I'm not perfect. I screw up every day, but I think that's what grace is all about."
—Tim Tebow

Nonbelievers must know that we are not claiming to be perfect when we share the gospel with them. Seeming to be too perfect can come across as self-righteous, and if we fail, we will come across as hypocritical. You do not have to be perfect to be an ambassador for Christ. You just have to believe in Him as your Lord and Savior. If you are doing your best to follow Christ and if God's grace has changed you, then so what if you will never be perfect. Who is better to share the gospel than you? There is no better ambassador.

We are therefore Christ's ambassadors, as though God were making his appeal through us. We implore you on Christ's behalf: Be reconciled to God (2 Cor. 5:20).

June 16: A God Who's There

Jesus tends to his people individually. He personally sees to our needs. We all receive Jesus' touch. We experience his care.
—Max Lucado

Our God is not a distant, abstract God, but He's a friend who sticks closer than a brother. He is a shoulder to cry on when we go through unexpected trials. He knows our issues, and He understands our pain. He is always close to the brokenhearted (Ps. 34:18), and just the sound of His name is a strong tower that we can run to whenever we need saving (Prov. 18:10). We can call on the name of Jesus at any time, and He will hear our prayers, comfort us, and give us peace.

He heals the brokenhearted and binds up their wounds (Ps. 147:3).

June 17: Run toward the Prize

When you are running toward Christ, you are freed up to serve, love, and give thanks without guilt, worry or fear. As long as you are running, you're safe.
—Francis Chan

We are always running one of two ways—either toward or away from Christ. We are never actually standing still because by doing so, we're effectively running away from Christ. We have to keep running every day with all we have toward Christ. We must throw off the weight of sin and shame so we are free to love intentionally and give generously and be able to share the gospel. When we give it all we've got, we know we are also running toward the heavenly prize that God has for us in heaven.

Let us lay aside every weight, and the sin which so easily ensnares us, and let us run with endurance the race that is set before us (Heb. 12:1 NKJV).

June 18: **Accuser of the Brethren**

To err is human; to forgive, divine.
—Alexander Pope

The Bible calls the enemy the accuser of the brethren because when you make a mistake, he constantly tries to remind us of it. Perhaps it is a voice in our heads when we wake up that says, "You're going to mess up today, just like yesterday." You then mope through the day wallowing in guilt. If you've repented of your sin, God has forgiven you. So remember to also forgive yourself. Don't listen to the enemy, or he will steal your joy. Shake off the defeat and walk in victory!

Therefore, [there is] now no condemnation (no adjudging guilty of wrong) for those who are in Christ Jesus, who live [and] walk not after the dictates of the flesh, but after the dictates of the Spirit (Rom. 8:1 AMPC).

June 19: **Exceedingly More**

God makes three requests of his children: Do the best you can, where you are, with what you have, now.
—African American Proverb

It is impossible for you to give 110 percent in everything you do because inherently you possess only 100 percent. In the natural, we have limitations. In the supernatural, God has none. So when you give your best every day, wherever you are, with the resources that are available to you, God will take care of the rest. He can do more with your talents, diligence, and perseverance than you ever imagined or dreamed of.

Now unto him that is able to do exceeding abundantly above all that we ask or think, according to the power that worketh in us (Eph. 3:20 KJV).

June 20: Giving Back

My father gave me the greatest gift anyone could give another person, he believed in me.

—Jim Valvano

My dad took me to my first Astros baseball game when I was 12 years old, and we went to many more after that. One day many years later, my dad wanted to pay for the Astros tickets and buy us dinner. I said, "Dad, I'm not in college anymore. I've got a job, so I can afford this." That didn't matter to him. He blessed me anyway. After all my dad has done for me, I couldn't wait to do something for him. So I purchased a very nice Father's Day gift, and because I was so excited about giving it to him, I did so a day early. Scripture teaches that God loves to give good gifts to his children (Matt. 7:11), and many of us can attest to all God has done for us. Therefore, let's pray that we will find ways to give back to God, remembering all He's done for us and assured that He will take care of our every need.

You must each decide in your heart how much to give. And don't give reluctantly or in response to pressure. "For God loves a person who gives cheerfully" (2 Cor. 9:7 NLT).

June 21: **All We Need We Already Have**

Do all the good you can, by all the means you can, in all the ways you can, in all the places you can, at all the times you can, to all the people you can, as long as ever you can.

—John Wesley

We often ask God to give us more. We want more resources, better opportunities, the right friendships, and more. But sometimes, we neglect to recognize that He may have already given us all we need. So before we ask for new blessings, why don't we ask God to show us how to maximize what we already have? Are you frugal or generous with your resources? Are there ways to make the most out of opportunities you already have? Instead of finding the right friends, how about being the right friend to someone? May we pray today to maximize all we currently have to the glory of God.

And God will generously provide all you need. Then you will always have everything you need and plenty left over to share with others (2 Cor. 9:8 NLT).

June 22: **Do All You Can**

If you can't do the good you would, do the good you can.

—Chuck Swindoll

People like to tell themselves all sorts of white lies. "If I had more time, I would spend more time with my family," or "If I made more money, I'd be more generous." Maybe it's this: "If she would put more effort into improving our marriage, I would, too." Often people have an all-or-nothing mentality that hinders them from living up to their God-given potential. Decide today to use all the time, money, and effort you can give to make a difference and be everything God has called you to be.

Do not withhold good from those who deserve it when it's in your power to help them (Prov. 3:27 NLT).

June 23: Man in the Mirror

> *I busted a mirror and got seven years bad luck,*
> *but my lawyer thinks he can get me five.*
> —Steven Wright

Others' perceptions and our perceptions of others' perceptions can often reflect how we see ourselves. Even if this reflection is positive, sometimes it does not change how negatively we feel about ourselves. Ultimately, when we look in the mirror every day, we have to like what we see. For this to happen, we must (1) mirror the life of Christ and (2) see ourselves through the unconditional lens of God's love. May we pray today to not allow the perceptions of others to distort how we see ourselves. May we see ourselves as God sees us, through the blood-bought love of His Son.

Anyone who listens to the word but does not do what it says is like someone who looks at his face in a mirror and, after looking at himself, goes away and immediately forgets what he looks like (James 1:23–24).

June 24: Speak No Ill

> *Speak ill of no man, but speak all the good you know of everybody.*
> —Benjamin Franklin

Too often people choose to gossip about someone else just because they can. You may have the juiciest information about someone and have all the power to cut them down to size and get even with them. Don't do it. When you decide to hold your tongue, eventually God is going to bless you in ways you initially may not foresee. Try this: Rather than finding something negative to say about a person you do not like, find something positive to say about that person. Use your energy for good and not for bad for two reasons: (1) people need encouragement, and (2) you need God's favor on your life.

So shall My word be that goes forth out of My mouth: it shall not return to Me void [without producing any effect, useless], but it shall accomplish that which I please and purpose, and it shall prosper in the thing for which I sent it (Isa. 55:11 AMPC).

June 25: Meditate on God

Thou hast made us for Thyself, O Lord, and our heart is restless until it finds its rest in Thee.
—Saint Augustine

Often people think that spending quiet time with God means reading their Bibles, praying, and writing in their journals. All of this is productive, but what if quiet time literally meant we are quiet? Sometimes, we can do nothing more productive than just stop and meditate on God. We might be surprised to learn that listening for the voice of God is a lot easier when we are not doing all the talking.

Be still before the LORD and wait patiently for him (Ps. 37:7 ESV).

June 26: Poor and Blessed

It was pride that changed angels into devils;
it is humility that makes men as angels.
—Saint Augustine

Ponder this question: Where would I be but for God? How we answer that will illuminate the depth of our spiritual maturity. Jesus said, "Blessed are the poor [the humble] in spirit, for theirs is the kingdom of heaven"

(Matt. 5:3 ESV). To be poor in spirit is a humble awareness that we were nothing more than dirty and malnourished beggars on the street corner asking for people's change before God rescued us so we could be sons and daughters of the King of kings and Lord of lords. We would be nothing and we would have nothing without God. But through Christ, we are royalty, and we inherit everything because of Him.

Humble yourselves before the Lord, and he will lift you up in honor (James 4:10 NLT).

June 27: Expecting Perfection from Friends

He that will have a perfect brother must resign himself to remaining brotherless.
—Italian Proverb

Peter did both great things and stupid things in his life. One stupid (and seemingly unforgivable) moment was when Peter denied that he knew Jesus. It happened while Jesus was in torment before He would be nailed to a cross. Peter might have done it to evade the same kind of fate. Jesus, however, forgave Peter because He never demanded perfection from Peter. Jesus knew that Peter had his flaws, as did all of His followers, but He saw Peter for what Peter could be—the one who would preach to thousands on the day of Pentecost and plant churches all over the world. Likewise, sooner or later, we are going to realize that our friends are not perfect. Our friends will let us down at times, but that does not mean they do not love us. They are not perfect, and neither are we. When we show them grace and forgiveness, we can expect the same in our less-than-perfect moments.

Forgive, and you will be forgiven (Luke 6:37).

June 28: **Walk with the Wise**

I'm a slow walker, but I never walk back.
—Abraham Lincoln

I once trained for a marathon with a guy who always stayed a step ahead of me. If I have learned anything about running, it is that we have to train with people who are faster than we are. If we want to become better, then train with the best. This concept also applies to wisdom. If we want to grow wiser, then we must not follow fools. Even if we already consider ourselves fairly wise, we need to spend time with people who are wiser than we are. God puts wiser people in our lives so they will take us further than we can imagine.

Walk with the wise and become wise; associate with fools and get in trouble (Prov. 13:20 NLT).

June 29: **Rejection**

I take rejection as someone blowing a bugle in my ear to wake me up and get going, rather than retreat.
—Sylvester Stallone

The word *no* is the hardest word to hear in the English language. After spending hours sending out cover letters and résumés, you wait for a call that doesn't come. You give your heart away, but the other person says, "Thanks, but no thanks." Like most people, you may not take no easily, but what will set you apart from most people is what you do afterward. Rejection either causes you to retreat to self-pity or use rejection as a stepping-stone to keep moving forward. You may be told no a hundred times, but all it really takes is one yes to change the course of your day and sometimes your destiny.

The righteous keep moving forward (Job 17:9 NLT).

June 30: **Role Player**

I pray to be a good servant to God, a father, a husband, a son, a friend, a brother, an uncle, a good neighbor, a good leader to those who look up to me, a good follower to those who are serving God and doing the right thing.
—Mark Wahlberg

Think of all the roles you play throughout your day: student, friend, brother, sister, son, daughter, employee, employer, mother, father, wife, husband, uncle, aunt, neighbor. Each of those roles presents a new ministry opportunity. Like Paul, we must strive to become "all things to all people" (1 Cor. 9:22). For one person, you may need to be a good listener; for another, a selfless servant; and for another, a sacrificial giver. Be all you can be to glorify your heavenly Father.

To the weak I became weak, to win the weak. I have become all things to all people so that by all possible means I might save some (1 Cor. 9:22).

July 1: **Everyday Surrender**

Let God have your life; He can do more with it than you can.
—Dwight L. Moody

It can be difficult to surrender ourselves completely to God because it's not a one-and-done or Sunday ordeal. It's an everyday affair. Just as Jesus asked the rich young ruler to sell all he had and give it to the poor to follow Him, sometimes God checks the true condition of our hearts by asking us to let go of something He knows we're putting above Him. The rich young ruler thought he could blaze a better trail for himself than God could, and that's why he just couldn't let go of his life. Sometimes, our hearts are no different than his. We want whatever it is we want. God wants us to surrender every aspect of our lives to Him—our time, our money, our relationships—leaving no box unchecked. When we do that, God can take us places we could never have gone on our own. Important question:

Is there something God is calling you to let go of today?

Peter began to say to Him, "Behold, we have left everything and followed You" (Mark 10:28 NASB).

July 2: Finding God's Will

When your will is God's will, you will have your will.
—Charles Spurgeon

Should I take that job or keep this one? Should I pursue this person, or should I wait? How can I better use my gifts to serve the church and my community? These kinds of questions are in essence asking the same thing: What is God's will for my life? Amazingly, our God is sovereign over the universe, and yet He takes time to care for the affairs of our individual lives. He knows us intimately, hears our prayers, and has a plan for us. God is often less concerned with our arriving at a particular destination than He is with who we are becoming along the way. God wants us to want His will. In other words, the launching point is when we ask, "Am I surrendered to God's will?" When God asks, "Who should I send?" our answer should always be how the prophet Isaiah responded: "Here am I. Send me!" (Isa. 6:8).

Teach me to do your will, for you are my God! Let your good Spirit lead me on level ground! (Ps. 143:10 ESV).

July 3: Savoring the Cinnabon

It is good to have an end to journey toward,
but it is the journey that matters in the end.
—Ernest Hemingway

One day, someone gave me a cinnamon roll from Cinnabon. If I have a vice in life, it is cinnamon rolls from Cinnabon! I inhaled it faster than you can say *sugar rush*. But like any delicacy, you should not inhale a Cinnabon. If you do, you will barely taste it. Eat it slowly, and savor every bite. Likewise, in life we can become so hyperfocused on a destination—graduation, promotion, marriage, retirement—that we neglect to enjoy the journey along the way. This life is your single Cinnabon, and it will taste sweeter if you learn to savor every bite.

Every good thing given and every perfect gift is from above (James 1:17 NASB).

July 4: Soul Detox

A vulcher looks for dead carcasses to consume every day, while the hummingbird looks for sweet nectar. Be a hummingbird.
—Craig Groeschel

So many of life's battles are fought in the mind. "I'm not good enough, I'm not smart enough, no one really cares about what I have to say." Negative thoughts make a negative person. People who want to remove unhealthy toxins from their bodies go on a cleanse because a healthy eater makes a healthy body. Christians must go on a soul detox. Let's ask God to identify and remove the critical, discontented, and fearful lies we've chosen to believe that keep us from God's purpose. Each day, we either choose to dwell on thoughts that bring death or bring life—the decision is ours.

Finally, brothers, whatever is true, whatever is noble, whatever is right, whatever is pure, whatever is lovely, whatever is admirable—if anything is excellent or praiseworthy—think about such things (Phil. 4:8).

July 5: **God Equips the Called**

What you are afraid to do is a clear indicator of the next thing you need to do.
—Ralph Waldo Emerson

There was a time when I was afraid to speak in front of people. It's fitting that in graduate school, God gave me a job as a speech coach to help students at the university in competitive public speaking. Needless to say, I had to get over my fear. I'm now quite often in the position to speak to various groups of people. For the past six years, I have taught public speaking at a local college. My plan was to avoid public speaking, but God's plan was for me to assume this responsibility for His purpose. Maybe there is something you're resistant to doing—teaching, serving, giving, loving—that God is calling you to do. You are afraid to do it. Step out in faith and assume responsibility. Throughout scripture, God never called the equipped but rather equipped the called. God will equip you to do what He calls you to do.

Don't be afraid, for I am with you. Don't be discouraged, for I am your God. I will strengthen you and help you. I will hold you up with my victorious right hand (Isa. 41:10 NLT).

July 6: **Keep Running Strong**

If it is important you'll find a way; if it is not, you'll find an excuse.
—Ryan Blair

When I set out to run long distances, sometimes my mind tries to tell me I should stop. "You may get hurt if you don't." "You've done good enough." Physically, I have found that I am capable of so much more, but it becomes a matter of leaping the mental hurdles so I can keep pressing forward. Perhaps God has called you to do something new, but it has become difficult and tiring to keep running toward it. Keep running strong. God will not call you to do something that He will not also give you the strength to complete. Pray for mental and physical strength to persist past the fatigue to reach what God has called you to.

I press on toward the goal for the prize of the upward call of God in Christ Jesus (Phil. 3:14 ESV).

July 7: Poise amid Dire Circumstances

I define poise as being true to oneself, not getting rattled, thrown off, or unbalanced regardless of the circumstance or situation.
—John Wooden

A roller coaster has its ups and downs, turns and twists—much like our day-to-day lives. When frustrations and disruptions make you spiral downward, hold on to the Lord, and He will keep you in perfect peace. Do not panic; pray for poise. Keep a level head, and play it cool. Circumstances can quickly change, but let your faith in Christ remain constant.

I am leaving you with a gift—peace of mind and heart. And the peace I give is a gift the world cannot give. So don't be troubled or afraid (John 14:27 NLT).

July 8: Climbing the Ladder

Management is efficiency in climbing the ladder of success; leadership determines whether the ladder is leaning against the right wall.
—Stephen Covey

What if firemen were afraid of heights? They wouldn't be able to save the lives of people above the first floor. What if CEOs were afraid of heights? They wouldn't get the wonderful skyscraper window office. What if pilots were afraid of heights? What takes only hours by plane would take days by car. Whatever ladder we climb in life, we need to make sure the ladder is resting firmly on heaven's doorstep. Circumstances cannot change if there is not something to climb and somewhere to go. Let us pray today that we will not be fearful of going higher if that is where God wants to take us. Let us pray that we always keep the ladder that we climb aimed in the right direction.

There was a ladder set up on the earth, and the top of it reached to heaven (Gen. 28:12 ESV).

July 9: **Defeated Christian**

> *A man is hindered and distracted in proportion*
> *as he draws outward things to himself.*
> —Thomas à Kempis

If the devil cannot defeat you, he will distract you. If you are guilt-stricken about the past, stressed in the present, and fearful of the future, then the devil has clouded your head with a lie. Repent and release your past to God, exhaling guilt and inhaling grace. Let go of stress and grab hold of the Savior. Give away fear, and expect God's favor. Pray today that you will focus on living by faith and that no fiery dart of the enemy will hinder you from moving forward in the direction God is calling you.

Set your minds on things that are above, not on things that are on earth (Col. 3:2 ESV).

July 10: **Work Is Worship**

Work becomes worship when you dedicate it to God and perform it with an awareness of his presence.

—Rick Warren

Perhaps you believe that your job does little to impact the world. Maybe you are a student who believes your schoolwork is insignificant. Perhaps you are an employee who does monotonous work for an overbearing boss or a parent who works tirelessly to raise thankless kids. Many Christians understand God as a distant, abstract force in the sky, working as if He had many more important things to do than watch you. This is not the God of the Bible. Christ is right beside you when you work. If most of us understood God that way, we would fall on our faces to praise Him and then work with more pep in our steps. Work would become worship, and very soon, your coworkers would say, "There's something different about that person."

Whatever you do, work heartily, as for the Lord and not for men (Col. 3:23 ESV).

July 11: **Break or Make**

First say to yourself what you would be; and then do what you have to do.

—Epictetus

Too many people say to themselves, "I wish I could, but—" The progression of that thought ceases in its tracks because they think it is too late to be what they might have been. They say I could, *but*—I'm too old, I don't have enough money, people will laugh at me, or I'm not talented enough. Which one do you say? Then, they are exactly who they have always been, completely dissatisfied and sometimes even cynical. It is natural to have some regrets in life, but don't ask what you could have done in the past; ask what you are going to do now. Everyone has failed at some point, and that often becomes an excuse. But it is what you do because of those failures that breaks you or makes you.

So whoever knows the right thing to do and fails to do it, for him it is sin (James 4:17 ESV).

July 12: **Know and Apply**

> *In all my perplexities and distresses, the Bible has never failed to give me light and strength.*
> —Robert E. Lee

I may know that I need to exercise, but knowing it is not enough. I have to move my muscles to produce results. What good is it to go to church each week to fill up on knowledge only to do nothing with it? It is not enough to know what we ought to do; we should do it. Give generously, talk right to your spouse, and help people who can do nothing for you in return. Apply the Bible. May we pray today to continue to learn the Bible while finding ways to apply it to our lives.

Our people must learn to do good by meeting the urgent needs of others; then they will not be unproductive (Titus 3:14 NLT).

July 13: **Desiring God's Will**

> *Real joy in life comes from when you get in the act of forgetting about yourself.*
> —Fred Smith

We often obey God but do so begrudgingly. We think, "Okay, I'll give my hard-earned money to the missionary, but he should get a job." Or we may think, "I will take care of the kids while my wife has a night out with her friends, but I'm not happy about missing out on the night I had planned for myself." God not only wants us to do His will, He also wants us to desire to do His will. Learning how to drive somewhere without using Google Maps is like practicing humility and selflessness to do God's will—both aren't easy initially. But eventually, the more we practice it, the more it becomes second nature. We may even find joy in doing it.

You need to persevere so that when you have done the will of God, you will receive what he has promised (Heb. 10:36).

July 14: Positive Framing

Always turn a negative situation into a positive situation.
—Michael Jordan

Maybe you are going through a negative situation right now, and people are saying you need to "think positively," as if replacing positive thoughts for negative ones is going to eliminate your very real problems. That only detaches you from reality. Instead, incorporate the concept of positive framing. That means you first acknowledge the negative situation in your life. For a situation you cannot change, you move on. For a situation you can change, you do something about it. If your framing is positive, then your situation can be, too. Pray today that you will know the difference and know how to handle the situations that arise.

Rejoice in hope, be patient in tribulation, be constant in prayer (Rom. 12:12 ESV).

July 15: **Serving with Right Motives**

Promoting self under the guise of promoting Christ is currently so common as to excite little notice.

—A. W. Tozer

Have you ever done the right thing but for the wrong reasons? I'll be the first to admit that I have. We may sincerely desire to serve God, but sometimes we do only as much as it benefits us. We may find ourselves using our talents and gifts primarily because there is something broken in us that desires personal recognition and praise. If God has given us talents and gifts to use for His glory, it's not wrong to use them, but we have to check our hearts daily to ensure our motives are right. The Apostle John described the Pharisees this way: "For they loved human praise more than praise from God" (John 12:43). The Pharisees weren't promoting God but only themselves. May this never be us. Sometimes, it may just not be the right season for us to use the full breadth of our skills since God may be calling us to serve Him in another capacity. It is important, however, to answer the call, because we may discover new capabilities we didn't know we had. It may also be true that the time may eventually come when we will use our talents and gifts in the way we'd always hoped for. In every season and situation, may we bring glory to God by making our motto like John the Baptist's: "He must become greater; I must become less" (John 3:30).

It's not good to eat too much honey, and it's not good to seek honors for yourself (Prov. 25:27 NLT).

July 16: Do Something

If you don't do your part, don't blame God.
—Billy Sunday

People often blame God for the darnedest things. "God has financially blessed everyone but me." God asks, "Why don't you find a higher-paying job?" Or you might say, "I don't have any friends at church." God says, "Join a Bible study." Or what about this: "God still hasn't put the right person in my life; that's why I'm single." God's reply might be, "You stay home every night and watch TV." (I do realize some are called to be single.) As the adage goes, God doesn't steer immovable objects. God will always do His part, but we must also do ours.

So I say to you: Ask and it will be given to you; seek and you will find; knock and the door will be opened to you (Luke 11:9).

July 17: Taking Risks

Don't allow any setback to become bigger than your comeback.
—Christine Caine

Most people who reach success in life had to take some chances in spite of uncertain circumstances. To find love, then, we have to put ourselves out there in spite of the possibility of getting hurt. Quitting a job to start a business is a risky endeavor because we may not earn money for a while—or ever, for that matter. We have to continually take risks to reap rewards, and past failures keep us from trying again. The disappointments and setbacks of life often cause us to settle, but settling can be a form of complacency, and complacency kills our comeback. What we neglect to realize is that it is a far greater risk to sit back and do nothing than to get up and do something. Let us pray today to ask God what risks He would have us take so we can realize His purposes for our lives.

To those who use well what they are given, even more will be given, and they will have an abundance. But from those who do nothing, even what little they have will be taken away (Matt. 25:29 NLT).

July 18: Audacity to Ask

If you have the audacity to ask, God has the ability to perform.
—Steven Furtick

Don't make goals you can achieve with little effort; that would actually be like making a grocery list. If you could do it without God, then there isn't much point in praying about it. Set goals you can only achieve by the power of a truly almighty God. The first step is daring to ask God for the impossible. Let us pray today to ask God to do what only He can do.

And since we know he hears us when we make our requests, we also know that he will give us what we ask for (1 John 5:15 NLT).

July 19: Your Lesser Self vs. Your Best Self

Make the most of yourself, for that is all there is of you.
—Ralph Waldo Emerson

Everyone has times that they are their lesser self, moments when they are not operating at their optimum. The lesser self discounts the hand of God and wallows in fear and self-doubt; however, the best self trusts that God will make a way where there seems to be no way. The lesser self hopes in earthly things, while the best self hopes in heaven above. The lesser self has a scarcity mentality; the best self has an abundance mindset. The lesser self stays in fear, while the best self walks by faith. By the power of the Holy Spirit, we can each be our best self, so today let us pray to make the most of ourselves and be all that God is calling us to be.

Therefore, if anyone is in Christ, he is a new creation. The old has passed away; behold, the new has come (2 Cor. 5:17 ESV).

July 20: A Godly Purpose

The purpose of life is a life of purpose.
—Robert Byrne

If I just took off running in any direction without planning my route or tracking my time, I would have no idea whether I was improving or where I was going for that matter. However, if I plan my route and set out to meet a particular time goal so I can beat a prior best time, then I have a purpose for my run. What is true for running is also true of our walk with God. If we start our days without ever stopping first to allow the Lord to speak to us, then we spiritually drift without direction. When we take the necessary time to stop for a few minutes each morning to be in prayer and in God's Word, then the Holy Spirit will lead us. We begin recognizing a godly purpose throughout our day. Perhaps instead of just saying "I will pray for you," we should actually stop to pray for someone. Maybe we could invite a coworker to lunch to share the hope we have in Christ. Let us pray today that our day will be filled with a godly purpose.

So I run with purpose in every step (1 Cor. 9:26 NLT).

July 21: Being Filled

Running is the greatest metaphor for life,
because you get out of it what you put into it.
—Oprah Winfrey

I have days that I do not feel very much like running. I go through the motions. My form is bad. Although going through the motions is still better than not running at all, I do not run to the best of my ability to reach my fullest potential. As Christians, we may have days that we do not feel much like being a Christian. We go through the motions in our prayer time. Our attitudes are bad. We are not operating to the best of our ability to reach our fullest potential. Just as a runner has to seek a second wind to keep running strong, a Christian must also seek the Holy Spirit to keep living strong. Let us pray today that Christ will fill us with His Holy Spirit. Living that way affects what we say, the way we live, our purity, and our faith. It is no longer just about how we feel but about being filled.

And the disciples were filled with joy and with the Holy Spirit (Acts 13:52 ESV).

July 22: Biblical Optimism

A pessimist sees the difficulty in every opportunity;
an optimist sees the opportunity in every difficulty.
—Winston Churchill

Optimism is more than a glass-half-full approach or finding the so-called silver lining. Biblical optimism is faith that God is still sovereign in spite of the difficulty of our circumstances. Through every difficulty, there is an opportunity to exercise biblical optimism. You may not always have clarity, but you will trust God. You probably will not always be happy, but your hope will be in Him. You may not always enjoy the pleasures of prosperity, but there is nothing that can steal your peace when God provides your every need. Pray today that you will have the faith to believe that God reigns sovereign over your circumstances.

And we know that in all things God works for the good of those who love him, who have been called according to his purpose (Rom. 8:28).

July 23: Choosing an Inner Circle

*The next best thing to being wise oneself is to live in a circle
of those who are.*

—C. S. Lewis

Who do you surround yourself with? While Jesus was a friend to sinners (he ate and fellowshipped with sinners in order to witness to them), Jesus's innermost circle of friends were his disciples Peter, James, and John, who shared His mission to be a witness to sinners. I think we'd all agree that people given to anger or drunkenness, who lie to their employer or spouse, or who cheat on their taxes are not the best options for an inner circle of friends. Like old comfortable shoes, sometimes we keep friendships out of convenience rather than making the hard decision to decrease our time with them or cut them off altogether. The Apostle Paul said, "Do not be misled: 'Bad company corrupts good character'" (1 Cor. 15:33). In other words, we eventually either upgrade or degrade to become more like those we spend the most time with. To grow in godliness and wisdom, we must choose an inner circle of friends who are striving to be godly and wise.

*Whoever walks with the wise becomes wise, but the companion of fools
will suffer harm* (Prov. 13:20 ESV).

July 24: Obeying God

One act of obedience is better than one hundred sermons.

—Dietrich Bonhoeffer

One of the hardest things you may ever have to do is say yes to God. Moses was called to go through a desert; David was called to fight a giant; and Jesus was called to die on a cross. Obeying God is not always comfortable, but it is never complicated. When God calls you, the right answer is yes anytime, anywhere, and for any reason. Ultimately, God will work mightily through you, just as He has anyone He has ever called.

For all of God's promises have been fulfilled in Christ with a resounding "Yes!" And through Christ, our "Amen" (which means "Yes") ascends to God for his glory (2 Cor. 1:20 NLT).

July 25: Christian Charity

Every charitable act is a stepping stone toward heaven.
—Henry Ward Beecher

A simple good-hearted act of charity is one of the most effective tools in our toolbox to share the gospel with others. As the adage goes, people do not care how much you know until they know how much you care. It does not have to be anything over the top, either. Perhaps it is taking them out for lunch after church or offering to babysit their kids so they can get a night out to themselves. Or maybe it's a prayer, hug, or smile to let them know you care. Paul told Timothy to teach the church this way: "Command them to do good, to be rich in good deeds, and to be generous and willing to share" (1 Tim. 6:18). Just a simple act goes a long way to soften hearts and minds so they are receptive to hearing the gospel.

And don't forget to do good and to share with those in need. These are the sacrifices that please God (Heb. 13:16 NLT).

July 26: A Gentle Answer

Apologetics, for this reason, is not merely about winning an argument. It is about winning souls.
—R. C. Sproul

We must regularly be in God's Word, looking for the answers to our questions so we can articulate the basis for our faith whenever opportunities arise. Additionally, the manner in which we share the gospel matters equally as much as what we say. First Peter 3:15 says, "Always be prepared to give an answer to everyone who asks you to give the reason for the hope that you have. But do this with gentleness and respect." Let me reiterate how Peter said we ought to do this with gentleness and respect, not condescension and rudeness. If the purpose of our study of apologetics is truly to win souls, then may others sense the love in our hearts before we give them the biblical knowledge of our minds.

Conduct yourselves with wisdom toward outsiders, making the most of the opportunity. Let your speech always be with grace, as though seasoned with salt, so that you will know how you should respond to each person (Col. 4:5–6 NASB).

July 27: What the Core Taught Me about Community

Every successful individual knows that his or her achievement depends on a community of persons working together.

—Paul Ryan

In 2014, while teaching residentially at Lone Star College, I began a young adult ministry called The Core. While I was officially called the advisor of the college club, I really acted like a pastor. My sister, Annelissa, was the president of the club. I invited my students, and she invited her friends. We had a lot of fun doing ministry together. She met her husband, Clayton, and I made lifelong friends, Jonathan and Luis, and was later a groomsman in their weddings. To this day, The Core continues, even after I handed it off to a local church. People have come to faith in Christ while making many new friendships in the process. What I learned is that in order for many people to grow spiritually, they need a community of people who will encourage them along their way. Even one meaningful friendship can be enough of an influence to completely change someone's spiritual trajectory in the right way. A community can be a source of encouragement when we go through hard times and a place where we can ask difficult questions about God and learn from the experience of others. It is a place where we can know people and be known by people. If you are not involved in any type of church community, get plugged in so people can pray for you and do life with you. Your faith will grow, and you will be more fulfilled when you are connected to other believers.

For where two or three are gathered in my name, there am I among them (Matt. 18:20 ESV).

July 28: Drawing Near to God

We need never shout across the spaces to an absent God. He is nearer than our own soul, closer than our most secret thoughts.
—A. W. Tozer

In the moments when we displease God by our sin, we need not feel as if He will abandon us. God knows the depths of our depravity, and yet He will never stop loving us or calling us into a right relationship with Him. God will not allow a true believer to ever be fully content living in continual sin. He first convicts them by way of the Holy Spirit so He can pursue their hearts and bring them back into fellowship with Him. We draw near to God by living as clean vessels, rooting out the sin in our lives, so we can see Him and hear His voice when we pray and read His Word.

Draw near to God, and he will draw near to you. Cleanse your hands, you sinners, and purify your hearts, you double-minded (James 4:8 ESV).

July 29: Work Willingly

Quality is not an act, it is a habit.
—Aristotle

At times, our work may be a monotonous grind, but scripture teaches that we must work willingly, not begrudgingly. That means we consistently show up on time, we're enthusiastic and positive, we get along with people, and we're willing to take on more tasks. Whether we realize it or not, we are not just honoring our companies by working willingly; we are also honoring Christ because more than likely, we cannot be good witnesses of Christ to others unless they see us as willing workers. Let us pray today to do quality work so it affords us the credibility to be a witness to our peers of what Christ did for us all on the cross.

Work willingly at whatever you do, as though you were working for the Lord rather than for people (Col. 3:23 NLT).

July 30: Self-Starter

Doing a little bit every day is a lot more important than doing a lot some day.
—John Maxwell

Many students are prone to procrastinating until the last minute. But they know they will eventually have to do the work in order to make the grade. It's a shame that the rest of life doesn't work that way. There isn't a teacher to hassle us to do little things we need to do. To fulfill our life's purpose, to bring a vision to fruition, or to turn a dream into a reality, we must make steady progress each day. Nobody is going to force us to do it. We have to be self-starters, and we just do it. That takes discipline. We may not have someday, but we do have today.

Here a little, and there a little (Isa. 28:10 KJV).

July 31: **Doubting and Inquisition**

Doubt is the incentive to truth and inquiry leads the way.
—Hosea Ballou

As Christians, it is normal at times to wrestle with doubt. Even atheists and agnostics doubt their disbelief. Everyone doubts. The difference between a skeptic and an inquisitor is that one is satisfied with only asking questions, while the other is searching for answers. May we never settle for anything but the latter. The interesting thing about searching for answers is that eventually, our questions yield answers and always more questions. And that's a good thing, because more questions lead to more answers. May we ask God in prayer to reveal the answers to us as we wrestle with doubt.

If you believe, you will receive whatever you ask for in prayer (Matt. 21:22).

August 1: **Delayed Obedience Is Disobedience**

When God is speaking, one word is more than enough. He's more interested in your full obedience than your total understanding.
—Steven Furtick

The prophet Samuel gave King Saul the word of God, asking him to completely wipe out the Amalekites (1 Sam. 15). Saul and his men kept the best of the spoils of the war for themselves. When Samuel asked Saul about this, Saul first tried to justify his actions. After Samuel rebuked him, only then did Saul do as God had asked. By then, however, it was too late. God's favor had already fallen from Saul, and God had given his throne away. There's a lesson to be learned: Delayed obedience is still disobedience. Be decisive in obeying God. Of course, God mercifully gives second chances, but isn't it better to get it right the first time? Don't delay. Be decisive.

Trust in the Lord with all your heart; do not depend on your own understanding. Seek his will in all you do, and he will show you which path to take (Prov. 3:5–6 NLT).

August 2: A Head Start

The prayer offered to God in the morning during your quiet time is the key that unlocks the door of the day. . . . Any athlete knows that it is the start that ensures a good finish.
—Adrian Rogers

There is something so beautiful about starting the day communing with God, sensing His presence, allowing Him to speak to you through His Word and in prayer to stir your heart for things that stir His. You get a head start on the day that you otherwise would not have unless you prayed. This change to your morning routine monumentally shapes your outlook for the rest of the day—what you do and say and in every way. You begin sensing God is guiding your every step like a good coach, speaking to you about how you can run your race with endurance and win. You start sharing your faith boldly, giving generously and loving intentionally. You live every day more purposefully.

And your ears shall hear a word behind you, saying, "This is the way, walk in it," when you turn to the right or when you turn to the left (Isa. 30:21 ESV).

August 3: Digging Deep

I would really love to go on an archaeological dig.
—Megan Fox

A few years ago, I participated in an archeological dig for artifacts left behind from an ancient Judean civilization dating back 2,200 years ago. When I got 50 feet down into the earth in the depths of a steep cave, I was thrilled to find a bone from a large animal and several pieces of pottery. Later, I was disappointed to learn that someone who had been invited to participate in the dig chose not to, simply because she did not want to get dirty. The reality is that this individual will never understand what she missed out on because she chose to stay at the surface. Telling her about this experience just isn't the same as her experiencing it for herself. There's a lesson to be learned. As soon as we get past reading the Bible on its surface, we begin to find treasures we otherwise never would have known about. God has more for you. Go deeper.

Search for them as you would for silver; seek them like hidden treasures (Prov. 2:4 NLT).

August 4: Loving God

The wrong way always seems the more reasonable.
—George A. Moore

Navigating from Jerusalem to Tel Aviv on my trip to Israel, I needed a plan. I spent an hour coordinating a bus route that would get me to a train that would get me to another bus that would get me to my destination. Within minutes of setting out on my journey, a local explained to me that I was doing it all wrong! I could simply take one bus straight to my destination. That way was less expensive and would save time. So that's what I did. That got me thinking: How many people spend their time trying to get closer to God the wrong way? They try to earn God's love through their own plan of being good (according to their standards), but when they fail, they feel miserable. Realize that not a single one of us can ever be good enough to earn God's love because we would have to be perfect. God has made an easier way for us: Simply accept the love He has freely given us through Jesus so we are free to love Him back. When you shift your focus from being good to reciprocating God's love, then goodness will happen a lot sooner, and so will becoming closer to God.

Whoever does not love does not know God, because God is love (1 John 4:8).

August 5: **A Word to the Weary**

A word of encouragement during a failure is worth more than an hour of praise after success.
—Unknown

Encouragement at just the right time, or "a word spoken in due season" (Prov. 15:23 KJV), can make your day and maybe even change the trajectory of your life. It's so important that we stay close to God and listen for His Holy Spirit to lead us with our words so we use them to bless others. You may have just the right word so they don't give up. God can use you in the course of your day, so pray that in and through you, He will have His way.

The Sovereign LORD has given me his words of wisdom, so that I know how to comfort the weary. Morning by morning he wakens me and opens my understanding to his will (Isa. 50:4 NLT).

August 6: **The Wounds of a Friend**

There is no love without forgiveness, and there is no forgiveness without love.
—Bryant H. McGill

When I played football in high school, I also learned how to play barber so I could cut my teammates' hair. One day, my buddy Matt asked me to cut his hair. I had always cut Matt's hair using regular scissors, but that day, I decided to use electric clippers to expedite the process. I clicked on the clippers, turned them on, and heard the buzz sound. Before I could blink, the attachment comb (the only thing keeping Matt's head from baldness) fell off, and so did a gaping chunk of his hair! Dumbfounded for a couple of seconds that felt like an eternity, I cringed in horror. Awkwardly, I chuckled, "My bad, bro." I gave Matt a $10 bill so he could pay a real barber to shave the rest of his head. Fortunately, Matt quickly forgave my mistake because he knew I had meant well. Hair grows back quickly, but our hearts take time, especially when our loved ones hurt us when they were "only trying to help." Scripture says that "faithful are the wounds of a friend" (Prov. 27:6 KJV) because we know they do love us even when they sometimes hurt us by the things they do or say. As a caveat, there are some people we should move on from after we forgive them. But generally speaking, we should forgive loved ones who have a general pattern of treating us well but neglect to say things just the right way or make boneheaded mistakes at times. That's so we keep our relationships with them intact and continue to learn and grow together.

Be kind to one another, tenderhearted, forgiving one another, as God in Christ forgave you (Eph. 4:32 ESV).

August 7: Joy in Sufferings

While other worldviews lead us to sit in the midst of life's joys, foreseeing the coming sorrows, Christianity empowers its people to sit in the midst of this world's sorrows, tasting the coming joy.
—Timothy Keller

While it may sometimes feel as if nobody can alleviate the pain and sorrow we go through in this life, as Christians we know that this suffering is only temporary because in the next life, we will know the joy of being with Jesus for all eternity. John wrote, "He will wipe every tear from their eyes. There will be no more death or sorrow or crying or pain, for the old order of things has passed away" (Rev. 21:4). We can simultaneously know this joy even in the midst of sufferings. Only Christ can give this joy, and in the midst of our tears, there is nothing that can steal it away.

For I consider that the sufferings of this present time are not worth comparing with the glory that is to be revealed to us (Rom. 8:18 ESV).

August 8: How Awesome Is This

My father did everything for me. He was awesome.
—Jenson Button

When God gave Jacob a dream at Bethel (Gen. 28), He promised to give Jacob the land on which he was sleeping, and He promised that his descendants would be blessed like never before. Jacob responded, "How awesome is this place!" (Gen. 28:17). Like Jacob, God wants to do something so amazing in our lives that only He could do it. Ask God to stretch your vision and increase your faith so in the end, your response to God will also be "How awesome is this!"

For the LORD Most High is awesome (Ps. 47:2 NLT).

August 9: Doubting Your Doubts

When in doubt, don't.
—Benjamin Franklin

When Jesus asked Peter to defy the laws of gravity by walking on water (Matt. 14), Peter's faith rose confidently one moment as He walked toward Jesus, but the next moment, his doubt made him sink into the ocean blue, and Jesus was his only rescue. Peter's faith probably looks as sporadic as ours does at times. In spite of Peter's doubt, however, God still used him in a mighty way to preach to thousands on the day of Pentecost and start churches to spread the gospel to the ends of the earth. It is little wonder why Peter's name means rock. Jesus said Peter was the rock on which He would build His church. As we face new challenges today and this week, we can turn to God for strength to overcome our doubts. Let us pray today to doubt our doubts, have faith, and live out our calling in the name of Jesus.

I tell you the truth, if you have faith and don't doubt, you can do things like this and much more. (Matt. 21:21 NLT).

August 10: Beauty for Ashes

Everybody wants happiness, nobody wants pain,
but you can't have a rainbow without a little rain.
—Unknown

Jacob served Laban for seven years to earn Rachel's hand in marriage, but after seven years, his future father-in-law tricked him and gave him Leah instead. Outraged, Jacob agreed to serve another seven years for Rachel, the one he truly desired. As Jacob also took Rachel to be his wife, this quickly became a difficult love triangle for Jacob, Rachel, and Leah to navigate. More often than not, Leah was the wife who felt unloved. Little did Leah know that Jesus would come through her lineage by way of Judah. Had she known that, she may have felt differently. Sometimes, we feel as though life has not been fair to us, but we fail to recognize that even in the midst of a mess, God is working all things in our lives for His purpose. God turns what would otherwise make us miserable and performs a miracle. He gives us beauty for ashes, and in Him, there is a hope and a future.

To give unto them beauty for ashes (Isa. 61:3 KJV).

August 11: **Knowing When to Quit**

Better three hours too soon than a minute too late.
—William Shakespeare

We're told to finish what we start. Sometimes, however, the book we're reading is not informative or the movie we've watched isn't very interesting. Maybe we've run into writer's block after having spent half a day writing a paper, or we have spent countless hours at time-sucking meetings. Sometimes, the best thing we can do is quit unimportant activities to free up time for the important. Let's ask ourselves this: "Am I busy just for the sake of being busy, or am I making effective use of my time?"

Making the best use of the time, because the days are evil (Eph. 5:16 ESV).

August 12: **Humbling Yourself**

Damn the torpedoes, full speed ahead!
—Admiral David Glasgow Farragut

When King David restored the Ark of the Covenant (the crown jewel and testament to God's glory) to Jerusalem after it had been taken by the enemies of Israel for many years, he ripped off all his royal garments and danced before the Lord (2 Sam. 6). His wife, Michal, scoffed since she did not understand how he could embarrass himself in such an undignified way. King David declared that he would become even more undignified in his pursuit of praising and honoring God. He was not above humbling himself before God. Likewise, there will always be people who want to criticize you for however you respond to God because they do not understand what God is doing in your life. Pray today that you will not be afraid to humble yourself and respond to God in spite of what others think.

Humble yourselves before the Lord, and he will lift you up in honor (James 4:10 NLT).

August 13: **Recoverability**

What psychologists refer to as recoverability is the process by which people regain functioning after a negative emotional event.
—Dr. Henry Cloud

Ruth had lost the one she loved and became a widow (Ruth 1). Life punched her in the gut and knocked her down, but she decided she wasn't going to stay down for the count. After Ruth grieved her loss, she chose to be faithful to God and worked hard to provide for herself and her mother-in-law. Instead of spending the rest of her life feeling sorry for herself, she stayed faithful where God had her at the time to serve her mother-in-law when she did not have to. Eventually, she embarked on new territory, and God gave her a husband named Boaz. How's that for recoverability? Life happens to us all. The key is how quickly we recover motivation, hope, judgment, and drive after something bad happens. Like Ruth, we have to embark on new territory so God can bless us.

That you would bless me and enlarge my territory! (1 Chron. 4:10).

August 14: **God Established Steps**

Write your plans in pencil and give God the eraser.
—Lenora Sundstrom

We should make plans, set goals, and have visions for what we want to do with our lives. That said, we shouldn't be so inflexible that we aren't reroutable to wherever God may be trying to lead us. In order for that to happen, we have to stay sensitive to the Holy Spirit, whom scripture refers to as God's still small voice. How do we stay sensitive to God's voice? We obey God in His Word by fighting sin, repenting, and seeking His forgiveness daily in prayer, finding accountability and wise counsel through community and by reading His Word daily. Sin separates us from God; however, He speaks to hearts that are surrendered and obedient to Him. "The LORD directs the steps of the godly. He delights in every detail of their lives" (Ps. 37:23 NLT). God may choose to take us to places we weren't expecting, but we will be most fulfilled when we are walking in step with Him.

We can make our plans, but the LORD determines our steps (Prov. 16:9 NLT).

August 15: Seeing the Unseen

Faith is to believe what you do not see; the reward of this faith is to see what you believe.
—Saint Augustine

In this life, we may never see God in a physical sense with our eyes; however, the Apostle Paul wrote that we can all see God in a spiritual sense with the eyes of our hearts. So what does that mean exactly? God always reveals Himself through the Bible, and He also chooses to reveal Himself uniquely to each of us if we are looking for Him. Perhaps it is a friend or pastor through whom God chooses to speak to our situations, or perhaps it is by way of a dream. Maybe it is overwhelming peace we feel after making important life decisions or by realizing answered prayers. These are a few of the many ways God strengthens our faith. The evidence of God is all around us; He will eventually reveal Himself if we are sincerely searching for Him.

The apostles said to the Lord, "Increase our faith!" (Luke 17:5 ESV).

August 16: **No Worries**

Worry often gives a small thing a big shadow.
—Swedish Proverb

Many people catastrophize the worst possible case scenarios, playing a series of what-ifs over and over again in their minds. "What if I never get married?" "What if I lose my job and then we lose the house?" "What if my loved one prematurely passes away?" I heard a statistic recently that 85 percent of what we worry about never happens. Nevertheless, that fact alone doesn't seem to stop us from worrying. We must always do as 1 Peter 5:7 instructs us to do. It says, "Give all your worries and cares to God, for he cares about you" (NLT). Once we do, that doesn't necessarily mean the worries quit coming, but we must continually choose not to hold onto them and to let go of them.

Don't worry about anything; instead, pray about everything. Tell God what you need, and thank him for all he has done (Phil. 4:6 NLT).

August 17: **Actions Speak Loudest**

Actions speak louder than words.
—English Proverb

From an early age, whenever I was passionate about something—sports, working out, or politics—I naturally created talking points to persuade people over to my side. Now, as someone passionate about sharing Christ with others, I have learned that it is usually not our innovative arguments that win others; it is our actions. When we treat people right, God will do the talking. He will work on their hearts in ways we cannot. Let us pray today that people will sense the love of God in us so He will be the one who does the talking by how we love.

Let us not love with words or speech but with actions and in truth (1 John 3:18).

August 18: Encourage Yourself

I know of no more encouraging fact than the unquestionable ability of man to elevate his life by conscious endeavor.
—Henry David Thoreau

There were low points in David's life when he felt like he did not have a friend in the world. There was no one to encourage him, but he encouraged himself in the Lord (1 Sam. 30:6). There will probably be low points in our lives when it may feel like no one is there to encourage us. It might seem like we are all alone. If you are low, do not stay there. Encourage yourself in the Lord by focusing on the many good things God has done for you with a belief that God will do this again.

[What, what would have become of me] had I not believed that I would see the Lord's goodness in the land of the living! (Ps. 27:13 AMPC).

August 19: Facing Trials, Passing Tests

The sooner we learn to be jointly responsible, the easier the sailing will be.
—Ella Maillart

One day, I joined some friends on a sailboat. The father owned the boat and had groomed his son to be able to take the reins of the boat eventually. That day would be the first time the son had to steer the boat on his own. Unexpectedly, we ran into a squall that rocked us to the point that the boat tilted on its side. To a newbie like me, it seemed as though we might crash into the pier. Never once, however, did the father stop believing in his son. In the end, the son passed the test with flying colors, and the proud father beamed with joy. Sometimes, our heavenly Father will allow us to face trials in order to test our faith. Even though your heavenly Father may not do everything for you, He is with you and stands ready to assist you. Just as this father looked at his son, so will your heavenly Father look at you, and you will come out stronger than ever before.

Be strong and courageous. Do not fear or be in dread of them, for it is the Lord *your God who goes with you. He will not leave you or forsake you* (Deut. 31:6 ESV).

August 20: Beautiful Within

Oh Lord, make me beautiful within.
—John Wooden

Each year, many billions of dollars are spent on big hair, spray-on tans, makeup, tummy tucks, gym memberships, and expensive retail. It is safe to say that both men and women spend quite a lot of time and money beautifying themselves on the outside, but are we spending the necessary time becoming beautiful on the inside? One of the best ways we could go about this is by asking God in prayer, "Lord, make me beautiful within." In other words, we are asking God to chip away at the character flaws in our lives that don't bring Him glory so we begin to exhibit character traits such as love, joy, peace, patience, kindness, goodness, longsuffering, gentleness, faith, modesty, temperance, and chastity (Gal. 5:22). It is not wrong to strive for outward beauty, but we must keep our efforts in proper perspective, recognizing that eventually, outer beauty fades. As we grow old and gray, it is actually inner beauty that is lasting.

So we do not lose heart. Though our outer self is wasting away, our inner self is being renewed day by day (2 Cor. 4:16 ESV).

August 21: **Expect the Best**

When you expect things to happen—strangely enough—they do happen.
—J. P. Morgan

Have you ever tried to pet a dog, only to have it flinch as you extended your hand? Perhaps the dog has been misused or hurt, so he doesn't realize you were only trying to be friendly and good to him. Likewise, sometimes people have a hard time believing our God is a good God who has good things in store for us. Scripture says that Jesus bore our griefs and sorrows (Isa. 53:4) so that we wouldn't have to. As we continue placing our faith in Jesus, we can expect good things from Him. Learn to expect the best.

The hopes of the godly result in happiness, but the expectations of the wicked come to nothing (Prov. 10:28 NLT).

August 22: **Walking by Faith**

The way you become brave, is one terrifying step at a time.
—Bryan McGill

Do you have a vision for what God has called you to do? It may seem lofty and terrifying at first glance. You may not see where the financing will come from. There may be people who said they would support you, and you wonder if they will actually do that. And you especially do not know what will happen if you fail. You think, "Perhaps I could be in an even worse position if I fail." These are all normal thoughts to have based on what you see in the natural. But if God has put a vision in your heart that you can only see by faith, then you have to trust that God is working on your behalf in the supernatural. Anything worth achieving will involve risk of failure because if it came too easily, it would not require faith. Trust that if God has called you to step out to walk with Him by faith, He will also provide for you every step of the way to see that vision to fruition.

I will instruct you and teach you in the way you should go; I will counsel you with my loving eye on you (Ps. 32:8).

August 23: **Nomads**

> *There's no place like home.*
> —Dorothy, *The Wizard of Oz*

I am one who loves to travel. I love everything about it—packing my suitcase, waiting for my flight in the terminal, sleeping in hotels, trying exquisite foods, meeting exotic people, and navigating a new city. But somehow, at the end of my trip, I cannot help but wish I were home. There is no place like home. As believers in Jesus on this earth, scripture says we are foreigners (Heb. 11:13). This earth is not our home; we are only passing through on our way to be with Jesus in heaven, our eternal home. Nothing this world can offer us can compare with the glory that Jesus will later reveal to us. One day, we will see that there really is no place like home.

They were looking for a better place, a heavenly homeland. That is why God is not ashamed to be called their God, for he has prepared a city for them (Heb. 11:16 NLT).

August 24: **A Good God**

> *There is no true gracefulness which is not epitomized goodness.*
> —Samuel Butler

As a child, I collected my town's police profile trading cards—150 in all. The police quickly became celebrities among the town's youth, and it was quite a spectacle to see parents chasing down police in their cars to get them to autograph the cards for their kids. Before the appearance of the police cards, many people had seen the police only from a distance, as enforcers of justice. Then, everyone got closer to the police and built a relationship with them, seeing their caring and good side. Similarly, God does not want us to see Him only from a distance as the enforcer of the law. Through grace, He wants us to see Him up close through Jesus as one who is good and cares about us.

The Lord is good to all, and His tender mercies are over all His works [the entirety of things created] (Ps. 145:9 AMPC).

August 25: Pit Bulls

Do right, and God's recompense to you will be the power of doing more right.
—Frederick W. Robertson

It was 8:00 a.m. one Sunday when I went for a jog. Twenty minutes later, I heard barking, so I looked behind me and saw two pit bulls on my tail. Startled, my mind raced for a getaway strategy. The pits seemed to smell my fear. I thought about kicking them and running for my life. Instead, I bent down and made kissy noises. The pits decided to be friendly, and they let me pet them. If someone has been after you with a hateful attitude, feeding off your fears and insecurities, decide to be the stronger one, and show them love and kindness. They just may change over time.

Don't let evil conquer you, but conquer evil by doing good (Rom. 12:21 NLT).

August 26: **Keeping Promises**

The only people with whom you should try to get even are those who have helped you.

—John E. Southard

David promised his best friend, Jonathan, that he would always show kindness to his family (1 Sam. 20:14–17). Jonathan's father was Saul, the angry king trying to kill David. Years later, when David became king after Saul and Jonathan died in battle, King David called for Jonathan's son, Mephibosheth, so he could bless him and keep that promise to Jonathan (2 Sam. 9:6). As God begins to bless you, never forget the people—friends, parents, and teachers—who have helped you along your way. Keep the promises you've made, remember to say thank you, and watch God continue to bless you.

Do to others as you would like them to do to you (Luke 6:31 NLT).

August 27: **Jaded by JNCOs**

Innovation distinguishes between a leader and a follower.

—Steve Jobs

Before skinny jeans were ever in style, there were JNCO jeans. When I was in third grade, everyone had a pair of those baggy, draggy, saggy jeans with a wallet chain. The gangster look was in. After repeated requests, I finally got my parents to get me a pair, but lo and behold, they suddenly went out of style. I was again not cool. I have since learned that there are two types of people: imitators and innovators. Imitators copy; innovators create. Imitators go where everybody has gone; innovators go where nobody has gone. I am not saying that you should not learn from those who have gone before you, because you should. But remember that many clones end up looking like clowns. In school-age years, it is normal to imitate—but when you grow up, it becomes time to innovate.

Do not be conformed to this world (Rom. 12:2 ESV).

August 28: Making a Difference

Be who God meant you to be and you will set the world on fire.
—St. Catherine of Siena

As a child, I attended my first Houston Astros baseball game with my dad. He took me down to the first base dugout to meet the pitcher, José Lima. In Norway, where I grew up, I had played soccer and hockey, but I didn't yet have an affinity for baseball. That was all about to change. Lima smiled at me, hugged me, and signed my baseball. Lima lit a fire in me, and from then on, I became a radical Houston Astros fan. For the next few years, I rarely missed a pitch. I memorized batting averages and the pitchers' ERAs. Baseball had previously just been a game that I knew little about, but Lima's kindness made the game personal for me. Likewise, do not underestimate your own ability to impact someone to come to faith in Christ. It may be as simple as an encouraging word, a smile, a hug, and a prayer. Believe that you are the chosen vessel that God will use to make a difference.

Let us think of ways to motivate one another to acts of love and good works (Heb. 10:24 NLT).

August 29: A Surrendered Heart

Faith is not the belief that God will do what you want.
It is the belief that God will do what is right.
—Max Lucado

A heart truly surrendered to God is one who says what the psalmist David said, "Create in me a clean heart, O God. Renew a loyal spirit within me" (Ps. 51:10 NLT). This act of surrender is not a one-time ordeal; it is an act that must be done daily. Whether it's the sins and regrets of our pasts, the hopes of our futures, or this very present moment, we must surrender everything to God. That includes our finances, our relationships, and our career ambitions, having faith that He can make more out of our lives than we could ever dream of. It does not mean that our faith will get us exactly whatever material and worldly things we want. Let's allow God to begin to change our heart's desires so we long for and take joy in the things He desires for us.

Take delight in the LORD, and He will give you your heart's desires (Ps. 37:4 NLT).

August 30: Writers Need Good Editors

To avoid criticism, do nothing, say nothing, be nothing.
—Elbert Hubbard

When I was nearly finished writing this book, I announced it on Facebook. Through Messenger, I became connected with Dawn and learned that she had been reading my daily devotionals online every day I had shared. She graciously offered to edit my posts for me, and she was a godsend. During the editing process, I quickly learned that if I edited the document myself, there were grammatical and fluency errors I unintentionally overlooked. As much as I tried, I could not spot my own errors as well as another set of eyes could. Writers need good editors. That is why I let a few people close to me help me. Those extra pairs of eyes pointed out the flaws that would have otherwise gone unnoticed, and they provided constructive criticism so my book would improve. Similarly, we need people in our lives who will point out bad mindsets and habits we are not recognizing. If we hold ourselves accountable to those people and allow them to examine our hearts, God can use them to provide constructive criticism and help us be all He has called us to be.

Better to be criticized by a wise person than to be praised by a fool (Eccles. 7:5 NLT).

August 31: Jealousy

Jealousy is the only vice that gives no pleasure.
—Anonymous

Jacob gave his son Joseph a coat of many colors, and Joseph's brothers became filled with jealousy. They tricked Joseph, sold him into slavery, and ripped his coat apart. They lied to Jacob and told him a wild animal had eaten Joseph. Perhaps the brothers had thought that acting on their jealousy would make Jacob love them more. But all it did was bring Jacob grief. Here is the lesson. Jealousy is not an indication of the potency of our feelings for someone; it is only an indication of our insecurities. Sometimes, we may deal with bouts of jealousy, but if we trust that our loved ones really do love us, we will not do anything to cause them harm or heartache.

A peaceful heart leads to a healthy body; jealousy is like cancer in the bones (Prov. 14:30 NLT).

September 1: Keep Swinging

Never allow the fear of striking out to keep you from playing the game!
—Babe Ruth

This was my moment. It was the eighth inning of the championship game, runners on second and third, we were down by a run, and I walked up to the plate. You see, I had grown up in Norway where my parents were missionaries, so when we came back to America and I joined a Little League baseball team, I did not have any experience. My passion for the sport was high, but my competency was low. I had become accustomed to striking out a lot that season, but thankfully, I had a supportive coach and team who never gave up on me. Now, the success of my team rested on my shoulders. The pitcher threw a high fastball. I swung with all my might and hit the ball deep into the outfield. Amazed, I watched it bounce off the scoreboard, driving in two runs to win the game and earn us the championship. The team jumped on me, howling my name, and for the first time that season, I felt like Babe Ruth. When attempting to achieve our goals, we often strike out. But we can't let it discourage us so much that we stop swinging. The more we practice, the better we will become, and eventually it will pay off. So keep swinging. Let us pray today that we will not give up doing what God has called us to do.

For the righteous falls seven times and rises again (Prov. 24:16 ESV).

September 2: **Transformed**

God uses ordinary people to accomplish extraordinary things.
—Unknown

As a child, I played with toy Transformers. At first glance, they were just grungy trucks and old station wagons, but I was fascinated to see how they could morph into super-machines that could do the incredible. I wished I could also morph into a superhuman who could help save the world. Only later did I realize that in Christ, my childhood fantasy could become a reality. It doesn't matter how average we think we are or how mediocre we feel, Christ can use us for His greater purpose. As soon as we allow Christ to begin to change the way we think about what we can do, we enable Him to morph us into someone new. When we are transformed and then believe in ourselves, Christ will use us in amazing ways.

Let God transform you into a new person by changing the way you think. Then you will learn to know God's will for you, which is good and pleasing and perfect (Rom. 12:2 NLT).

September 3: **Faithful in Small Things**

Be faithful in the small things because it is in them that your strength lies.
—Mother Teresa

A faithful Christian life usually does not consist of mostly mountaintop moments where we are acknowledged in some grand way for our faithfulness. Rather, it is a life filled with what might seem like monotonous moments for which we are never recognized. Your strength lies in staying faithful in the *small* things such as your quiet time alone with God every morning, tucking your children in at night, or telling your spouse you love them. It is *small* things such as sharing the gospel with just one more person, calling someone who is hurting, or showing up to your Bible study on a weekday night when you are tired from a long day at work. I emphasize *small* because obviously, these things are not unimportant, even though they often go unseen. It is just like the foundation of a home, which is important although it, too, goes unseen. The small things are the foundational things on which we must build our lives—the things that will ultimately make life well-lived.

Whoever is faithful in small matters will be faithful in large ones; whoever is dishonest in small matters will be dishonest in large ones (Luke 16:10 GNT).

September 4: **Endurance in Hard Times**

Endurance is not just the ability to bear a hard thing,
but to turn it into glory.
—William Barclay

Sickness and disease, the death of a loved one, a betrayal by a friend, a company layoff, bills that pile up, a miscarriage, a child bullied at school, separation and divorce—life can be hard and sometimes excruciatingly so. There are no easy answers for why God allows hard things to happen, and there usually isn't much anyone can say to alleviate our pain. We must remember that Christ, too, suffered even unto the point of death. Yet Christ prayed to the Father, saying, "Please take this cup of suffering away from me. Yet I want your will to be done, not mine" (Luke 22:42 NLT). Following Christ never meant we would always be comfortable. But, like Christ, we can allow God to produce enduring character through suffering. So how will we respond to hard things? We ought to pray for deliverance, but it's just as important to pray that we glorify God in every situation.

We rejoice in our sufferings, knowing that suffering produces endurance, and endurance produces character, and character produces hope (Rom. 5:3–4 ESV).

September 5: Taking Care of the Body

Take care of your body. It's the only place you have to live.
—Jim Rohn

In 2013, I had an ailing shoulder that debilitated me so I couldn't work out at the gym effectively. My shoulder was not just a shoulder problem; it also affected whether my chest, back, biceps, and triceps could perform the workout. Never before did I more painfully realize that the body is connected. The church (and the people in it) is the body of Christ (1 Cor. 12:26); it is a team. I have learned from working on various teams that when one person on the team hurts, it can affect how the rest of the team performs. If you are part of a team—church, school, marriage, work—pray today that you will be able to recognize when someone is hurting so you can encourage them and help restore them to health. You will need that teammate to recover quickly so your team (the body) will function as it should.

Therefore encourage one another and build each other up, just as in fact you are doing (1 Thess. 5:11).

September 6: Just Worship

The more you worship, the less you worry.
—Rick Warren

Throughout the most agonizing seasons of King David's life—running from his enemies, fighting sin, losing his loved ones—he worshiped God in spite of his pain. He played the harp, danced, and sang. He was the Bon Jovi of his time! I've learned throughout my short life that in the midst of painful seasons, I also have to worship God, although in my own way. I write! And I write with all my heart. Maybe you are a teacher, physician, athlete, or technician. Whatever it is you do, worship God through it, especially when you might be hurting. Just like God brought David through his pain, He will do the same for you.

Give to the LORD the glory he deserves! Bring your offering and come into his presence. Worship the LORD in all his holy splendor (1 Chron. 16:29 NLT).

September 7: Trusting God with Your Future

Never be afraid to trust an unknown future to a known God.
—Corrie ten Boom

Where am I going to get the money to pay for this? What am I going to do now? I cannot believe this happened to me. I really thought they were the one. Can I catch a break for once? We often do not have the answers to some of life's difficult questions or uncertainties, but comfort and peace come in knowing the One who does. What we tend to want from God is clarity, but He simply wants us to trust Him. When Jesus's disciples were anxious about His leaving them to ascend to heaven, Jesus said, "I am leaving you with a gift—peace of mind and heart. And the peace I give is a gift the world cannot give. So don't be troubled or afraid" (John 14:27 NLT). As believers in Christ, we have that same gift, the Holy Spirit in us, to bring us peace. In other words, Christ never left us because He now resides in us. He is with us.

When I am afraid, I put my trust in you (Ps. 56:3).

September 8: Following Jesus

> *No man can follow Christ and go astray.*
> —William H. P. Faunce

At the age of five, I decided I wanted to follow Christ by giving up what I enjoyed the most. That happened to be the very worst thing I was doing: watching *Power Rangers* and karate kicking my sisters! It is not that there was anything so inherently wrong with the hit TV series, but it had become something I was so obsessed with that I had put it before God, and it affected how I interacted with others. By giving up *Power Rangers*, I decided to surrender my heart completely to Christ, removing what I now see was an idol in my little life. I asked my dad, a minister, to baptize me that very day, which became a turning point in my life. For most of us, idols do not come to inhabit our lives by way of a TV series, but perhaps our idol is an unhealthy amount of importance we place on a relationship, a career, a goal, or a dream. Quite simply, we get sidetracked from following Christ by following our own desires, wherever they may lead us. These things are not inherently evil, but they become idols if we put them before God. We must prayerfully ask ourselves, "What inhibits me from following Christ and becoming all He means for me to be?"

Then Jesus said to his disciples, "If any of you wants to be my follower, you must give up your own way, take up your cross, and follow me" (Matt. 16:24 NLT).

September 9: **Joyful Repentance**

Fear-based repentance makes us hate ourselves.
Joy-based repentance makes us hate the sin.

—Tim Keller

A bride and a groom seek to please and be faithful to one another, not out of the fear of divorce if they fail to, but from a pure joy they find in loving one another. The Bible refers to Christians as the bride of Christ, and we, too, must seek to please our Groom (Eph. 5:32). There will be times throughout the relationship that we fail our Groom because of our sin, but He loves us with an agape love that is sacrificial and unconditional. It is because of this love that we ought not to repent of our sins out of begrudging obedience, but rather out of the joy we find in pleasing a Groom who has been infinitely good to us.

When anxiety was great within me, your consolation brought me joy (Ps. 94:19).

September 10: **Heaven Above**

Has this world been so kind to you that you should leave with regret?
There are better things ahead than any we leave behind.

—C. S. Lewis

When we stay in a hotel room, we cannot become too comfortable because we are there for only a short time. It's not home. This world we inhabit is a hotel room because everything here is temporal, and we are merely passing through on our way to eternity. No matter how kind the world has been to you, it cannot compare to the glory that awaits you in heaven, where we will walk on streets of gold to meet and worship Jesus. Let us pray that we will live today and each day with eternity in mind, not caught up in things that will pass away but rather in things that are truly lasting.

Think about the things of heaven, not the things of earth (Col. 3:2 NLT).

September 11: **Live to Give**

The high destiny of the individual is to serve rather than to rule.
—Albert Einstein

Jesus—the Son of God, the King of kings and Lord of lords, the Savior of the world, the Creator of the universe—washed his disciples' feet. The statement He made was vividly clear: He was there to serve. Jesus set the example for us to follow. What better model do we have than to follow His lead by serving others? Start by serving your family and friends. Serve your community and church. Serve someone who can do nothing for you in return. When you do, just watch as your paradigm begins to shift from inward to outward. You'll start to see how this adage is true: It's a blessing to be a blessing. When you live to give, then God will give back to you.

Give, and it will be given to you. A good measure, pressed down, shaken together and running over, will be poured into your lap. For with the measure you use, it will be measured to you (Luke 6:38).

September 12: **Eat Up**

"Come and dine," the Master calleth, "Come and dine."
—C. B. Widmeyer

When I started lifting weights, I was 15 years old, 110 pounds, with an earnest zeal for becoming a bodybuilder! I woke up at 5:00 each morning to lift with my football teammates before classes began. After a couple of weeks, I realized that although I had pushed myself through exhausting workouts, I had not grown much muscle or increased my strength. I found a big guy at the gym and asked what he did to get big. After comparing his strategy with mine, I realized that our diets were different. I ate what I wanted; he ate what he needed. He intentionally ate certain calories—complete proteins, complex carbohydrates, polyunsaturated fats, vitamins, and minerals—that properly nourished his body so he could grow in strength and size. Because I did not plan my meals, I often skipped meals and became malnourished. So I adjusted my diet and began eating right to see the changes in strength and size that I hoped for. I grew. In the same way, how many people desire to grow spiritually, and although they go to church, they fail to nourish their lives with God's Word and prayer? Let the prayer of our hearts be that we will nourish our lives with prayer and God's Word. Let's eat up.

Blessed is he that shall eat bread in the kingdom of God (Luke 14:15 ASV).

September 13: Speaking Truth in Love

People may hear your words, but they feel your attitude.
—John C. Maxwell

The expression goes, "It's not what you say but how you say it." If we speak truth into someone's life, especially when we confront another believer about their sin or share the gospel with an unbeliever, it's important that we do it with the right attitude. May we not have an attitude of self-righteousness and condescension but one full of grace and love. Let us pray that God gives us the right words to say and that His heart is behind our words so more people may come to know God in His fullness and live their lives to bring Him glory.

Do nothing from selfish ambition or conceit, but in humility count others more significant than yourselves (Phil. 2:3 ESV).

September 14: **Candy Bar Christian**

Problems can become opportunities when the right people come together.
—Robert South

In grad school, it was my dream to go to Israel to walk in the footsteps of Jesus, but the problem was that I didn't have the money to go. That's when my buddy Seth suggested I sell candy to earn the money. At first I thought, "What do I look like, a Girl Scout?" But then we leveraged Seth's Sam's Club membership to purchase candy bars, cookies, and gummy worms and brought them back to the school to sell them at a cost cheaper than vending machines. Fortunately for me, I was selling candy at a university that was once a Baptist seminary, and I wanted to go to the Holy Land during finals when students needed a sugar rush. I raised more than enough money. When those students learned where I wanted to go, they blessed me more than I could have dreamed. For a few days, I was called Candy Bar Christian. I had just as much fun raising the money as I did visiting Israel. What I learned from this experience is that we can have a vision for where we want to go, but often we can't get there if we don't have people who help us fine-tune and carry out our vision. God's favor always flows through people, and we need to elicit their help to get wherever we are called to go.

As iron sharpens iron, so one person sharpens another (Prov. 27:17).

September 15: **Forgiving Our Loved Ones**

It is easier to forgive an enemy than to forgive a friend.
—William Blake

Sometimes, the cost of forgiveness is small when we have invested little, but it is great when we have invested much. Unanswered questions and what we wish we had said bombard our minds. "How could you?" "I was there for you." "I'd never have treated you the way you treated me." Maybe a relationship is damaged beyond repair, but we must choose forgiveness anyway—not for their sake but for ours. Maybe the relationship is one we want to reconcile, and in that case, give them the chance to work the situation out with you. Perhaps they were 95 percent wrong, and we were only 5 percent wrong (if that). We can still apologize for however we were wrong. A truly fulfilled life will not be one lived without forgiveness. Let us pray today that we will do as Jesus asked Peter to do in Matthew 18:21–22—to forgive 70 times seven so we can do our best to be at peace in our relationships.

Bear with each other and forgive one another if any of you has a grievance against someone. Forgive as the Lord forgave you (Col. 3:13).

September 16: Gratitude for Little Blessings

Human felicity is produced not so much by great pieces of good fortune that seldom happen, as by little advantages that occur every day.
—Benjamin Franklin

One of the practices I do every day is write down 10 things I am grateful for because I don't want to forget the little blessings I could otherwise take for granted. It could be as simple as writing this: the clean air I breathe, food in my belly, clothes on my back, a car to drive, a roof over my head, a country that is free, health in my body, my family and friends who love me, my job that affords me a living, a church to attend. Even if you don't have everything you want in life, the things you do have are worth being thankful for. Pray today that you will be someone who expresses gratitude, writing blessings down every day if you have to, and definitely giving thanks to God in prayer and saying thank you to the people who bless you.

O give thanks to the Lord, call on His name; make known His doings among the peoples! (1 Chron. 16:8 AMPC).

September 17: Enjoying Today

Learn how to enjoy where you are on the way to where you're going.
—Joyce Meyer

What delays your joy? Do you have to graduate from college first? Land a higher-paying job? Find the right person? Have kids? Have grandkids? Retire ASAP? You see, if you're not careful, you can become so hyperfocused on where you're headed that you fail to enjoy the journey along the way. The Apostle Paul learned to find contentment in whatever state he was in (Phil. 4:11–13), even while he was in prison. So at the very least, we can enjoy today even if not everything in our lives is going our way. Let us prayerfully ask God to help us find balance between contentment and ambition so we find joy in today.

For the joy of the LORD is your strength (Neh. 8:10).

September 18: Chosen by God

Whatever I will become will be what God has chosen for me.
— Elvis Presley

With God, it does not matter which side of the tracks you were raised on, how much money you make in a year, or who your friends are. God does not care what you look like, how old or young you are, or how good or bad your résumé is. Throughout history, God has chosen ordinary people to accomplish the extraordinary. God chose David, a shepherd boy, to be king. God chose Elisha while he was plowing in a field to be a prophet. Jesus chose a group of fishermen, a tax collector, and societal nobodies to be disciples who would change the world. It did not matter what others thought of them, because God had chosen them. Prayerfully believe that because God saved you, you are chosen by Him for plans that are much greater than simply living for yourself. Rest assured that when God saved you, He had plans to use you.

Isn't it obvious that God deliberately chose men and women that the culture overlooks and exploits and abuses, chose these "nobodies" to expose the hollow pretensions of the "somebodies"? (1 Cor. 1:28–29 MSG).

September 19: Debt-Free

A man in debt is so far a slave.
—Ralph Waldo Emerson

Imagine every debt that is unpaid. For some, it is a student loan or a credit card debt. For others, it is medical bills, a car loan, or a mortgage. Our sin is also a type of debt, and the Bible says, "The wages of sin is death" (Rom. 6:23). That is the only way our sin debt could have been paid. Jesus paid that sin debt. He was God's gift to us when Jesus took on the sins of the entire world and died in our place so we could be debt-free. Wherever you are in your relationship with God today, do not carry this debt any further on your own. Simply confess your sins to God, repent, and ask to be in a right relationship with Him. By God's grace, you can be debt-free.

For by grace you have been saved through faith. And this is not your own doing; it is the gift of God (Eph. 2:8 ESV).

September 20: Overcoming Weaknesses

Admitting your weaknesses does not diminish your strengths:
it shows your courage.
—Erin Andrews

In some job interviews, the interviewer asks candidates about their weaknesses to hear how they talk about themselves. The interviewer can then assess whether or not they are a fit for the company. To cover up their weaknesses in hopes of impressing the interviewer, candidates learn to say something like this: "I work too hard because I'm a perfectionist." That might be the best way to answer the question in a job interview, but it is not the best approach for having an honest conversation with God regarding spiritual weaknesses. If we are dishonest with God about our weaknesses and neglect to repent of our sins and ask for forgiveness, we are only fooling ourselves. We must remember that God already knows our weaknesses and loves and accepts us in spite of them. Let us go to God in prayer today, asking Him to search our hearts to bring our weaknesses to our attention so we can overcome them by the grace and strength only God can give.

My grace is enough; it's all you need. My strength comes into its own in your weakness (2 Cor. 12:9 MSG).

September 21: **Reading You**

Whenever you do a thing, act as if all the world were watching.
—Thomas Jefferson

People may not take the time to read the Bible, but they will read your life. Ask yourself this: In my day-to-day interactions, do I demonstrate Christ? Do I show others love, grace, kindness, and selflessness? Am I diligent, punctual, and honest in my work? Do I exhibit the peace known only by faith and trust in God? These might be a good litmus test for you. If the results come back positive, then continue doing what you're doing. But if the results come back negative, then ask Christ to help you change. This isn't just about you being your best each day; it's also about others coming to know Christ by watching you.

Let every detail in your lives—words, actions, whatever—be done in the name of the Master, Jesus, thanking God the Father every step of the way (Col. 3:17 MSG).

September 22: **Spiritual Realignment**

*True freedom is where an individual's thoughts and actions are in
alignment with that which is true, correct, and of honor—
no matter the personal price.*

—Bryant H. McGill

If you have ever driven a car that needed realignment, you'll know that
no matter how hard you tried to keep the car straight, it will veer to the
left or to the right. This is also true for a life not led by the Spirit. We
veer because we are steered by our flesh. We know this might be the case
due to certain indicators, and while there could be more, here are a few.
Perhaps we have not sensed God's presence in a long time. Maybe we do
not enjoy a sense of purpose we once had. Somehow along the way, we
lost our passion for serving others. Whatever the case, everyone, no matter
who they are, is in need of a spiritual realignment at times. Let's ask God
in prayer today to go to work on our hearts so we will be led by the Holy
Spirit to be realigned with God's will. The best path to take is always the
straight and narrow path. So let's go!

So I say, walk by the Spirit, and you will not gratify the desires of the flesh
(Gal. 5:16).

September 23: **Don't Stop Loving People**

*I'd realize it's not worth our time to worry. You do your best,
and God will put the right people in your path.*

—Taya Kyle

At times, we have all invested our love in people who have not properly
reciprocated our love. Maybe your child has gone wild, or a friend has
grown distant, or a coworker belittles you behind your back. In spite of
this, we cannot allow ourselves to grow cold or cynical to the point that
we stop loving people. We must keep loving people. We must trust God

to put the right people in our lives who will appreciate our love and love us back.

So let's not get tired of doing what is good. At just the right time we will reap a harvest of blessing if we don't give up (Gal. 6:9 NLT).

September 24: **Follow the Peace**

It does not take much strength to do things, but it requires a great deal of strength to decide what to do.
—Elbert Hubbard

God gives us the Holy Spirit so we can discern which direction we ought to go in those times we do not know what to do. That means we are never alone. God is our strength and counselor. In prayer and meditation, He will lead you. I have learned that it helps to act as if I had already made my decision to see how I feel. I recommend that you prayerfully try doing the same before you have to make an important decision. Do you have peace about it? If not, that might be an indicator that it's not the right decision. Follow the peace.

Do not be anxious about anything, but in everything by prayer and supplication with thanksgiving let your requests be made known to God. And the peace of God, which surpasses all understanding, will guard your hearts and your minds in Christ Jesus (Phil. 4:6–7 ESV).

September 25: **Maximize to Multiply**

*A dream doesn't become reality through magic;
it takes sweat, determination and hard work.*
—Colin Powell

Jesus tells a parable of three servants whose master gives each of them varying amounts of talents (currency). The master gave the first servant five talents, the second servant two talents, and the last servant one talent. I want you to imagine that the material talents the master gave them are just like the unique talents and abilities that God gives us. The first and second servants receive their amounts, and then the second servant could have said, "You gave him more, so I'm not going to do anything." Instead, he maximized what he was given and multiplied it. The third servant, however, did something remarkable. He buried his talents because he believed the master was a harsh man. He received the least talents, so he thought it would be better to not even try. What if his one talent could have made him the next Michelangelo? A Nobel Peace Prize winner? We will never know. Sometime in his life, he let his dreams die because he no longer believed in himself. The master could do nothing with him, but to the first two he said, "Well done, my good and faithful servants" (Matt. 25:23 NLT). God did not give us our talents and abilities to bury them. At the end of our lives when we stand before God, we also want to hear Him say, "Well done." Light a fire in your belly and dream again. Maximize whatever God gives you so you multiply it.

The master said, "Well done, my good and faithful servant. You have been faithful in handling this small amount; so now I will give you many more responsibilities. Let's celebrate together!" (Matt. 25:23 NLT).

September 26: Invest the Whole Heart

Let us not be satisfied with just giving money. Money is not enough, money can be got, but they need your hearts to love them.
—Mother Teresa

Jesus and his disciples were in the Temple watching the Pharisees as they gave large sums of money. There was also a poor widow who gave two mites. Jesus said the widow had given the most because she had given all she had, and the Pharisees had given out of their abundance. This story is not just a lesson to inform us how we should give our finances to God and others, but it is also about how we invest our whole hearts by loving God and others. Do not compare what you can give to what others are giving; just do the very best you can, even if on the surface it does not appear to be all that much. God sees the heart, and when you invest the whole heart instead of just a part, He is smiling down on you, and your reward will come from the Lord. Pray today that you would love more intentionally by serving God and others sacrificially and by giving whatever you can give.

For they have given a tiny part of their surplus, but she, poor as she is, has given everything she has (Luke 21:4 NLT).

September 27: **Starting the Day Right**

How you begin your day will frequently determine how you end it.
—Woodrow Kroll

Learning to start our days in prayer and in God's Word can greatly improve the quality of our days because God can begin to inform our decisions. When we read God's Word, we learn what God has said so we can know what to do. When we are talking to God in prayer, we can tell Him anything and everything on our minds. When we're quiet, He begins to form impressions on our hearts. From this, God can give us a peace that will surpass all understanding, and we can know what to do based on listening to that peace. It is more likely that we can end our days in peace if we start it that way.

Call to me and I will answer you, and will tell you great and hidden things that you have not known (Jer. 33:3 ESV).

September 28: **Stick-to-it-ivity**

Perseverance is failing 19 times and succeeding the 20th.
—Julie Andrews

Before Abraham Lincoln won the presidency, he had failed a total of seven times in his bid to become an elected official. Thomas Edison failed more than 10,000 times before he successfully made the light bulb, but it was on his last attempt that he succeeded. Oprah got fired from her first job as a TV reporter because she was "unfit for TV," and now she has her own TV network that is fittingly called OWN. The question I pose to you is simple: Are you willing to fail? Like anyone who has ever attempted to do something great, learn to look at failure as a progression of a process. Failure does not have to be a stumbling block; it can be a stepping-stone to success. Pray today that you would have stick-to-it-ivity to persist past failures and realize the God-given purpose for your life.

Do not grow weary in doing good (2 Thess. 3:13 ESV).

September 29: **Tale of Two Kings**

There are two kinds of people: those who say to God, "Thy will be done," and those to whom God says, "All right, then, have it your way."
—C. S. Lewis

Saul was chosen to be King of Israel, and while he served God for a short time, he did not over the long haul. God chose David to replace Saul as king, and although David was not perfect either, he served God for his entire life. As a result, Israel prospered, and David's lineage produced Jesus, the King of kings, about 1,000 years later. Here is my point. When we choose to live for God, there are both short-term and long-term benefits. The sacrifices you make now are not in vain; they will pay off for you and your children and grandchildren, too.

Commit your actions to the LORD, and your plans will succeed (Prov. 16:3 NLT).

September 30: Standing in Hope vs. Walking by Faith

There's a big difference between standing in hope and walking in faith.
—Steven Furtick

Standing in hope will not bring the vision God has given me to pass, nor will it yours. You can be hopeful and also stagnant. But faith does not diminish God's will to divine chance. It doesn't say, "If it's going to happen, it will happen." No, faith is a course of action to take what God has already given you. Even when fear sets in to cripple you, walking by faith means listening for God's voice and obeying Him every step of the way. Pray today that you will be proactive in carrying out the calling God has placed on your life.

For we walk by faith, not by sight (2 Cor. 5:7 KJV).

October 1: Living Like Sheep

If thou art wise thou knowest thine own ignorance;
and thou art ignorant if thou knowest not thyself.
—Martin Luther

Throughout the Bible, the followers of Christ are compared to sheep. I hope this does not offend you, but sheep are inherently dumb animals. If they aren't kept with their flock under the protection of their shepherd, they wander astray only to fall and become unable to pick themselves up and to eventually be killed by a predator. We are no more fortunate when we wander. Proverbs 14:12 says, "There is a way that appears to be right, but in the end it leads to death." Frank Sinatra may have appeared to have success when he sang, "I did it my way," but we as followers of Christ are called to live keenly aware of our own limitations. We must know that our way is wrong and leads to death, and God's way is right and leads us to life.

For you were straying like sheep, but have now returned to the Shepherd and Overseer of your souls (1 Pet. 2:25 ESV).

October 2: Giving God Our Dreams

It takes a lot of courage to show your dreams to someone else.
—Erma Bombeck

Pharaoh set out to kill every Hebrew baby boy in Egypt. Moses's mother decided to save Moses by putting him in a basket of papyrus reeds to float him down the Nile River. Of course, her dream was to keep her baby and watch him grow big and strong; however, all she could do was trust God as she gave her dream over to Him. By God's providence, Pharaoh's daughter found Moses and raised him herself. Moses grew to be the man who led the Jews out of captivity in Egypt. Life can feel like a constant tug-of-war between what we want and what God wants. Like Moses's mother, we must also give God our dreams and trust Him. That's when He will begin to do more amazing things in and through our lives than we could have ever hoped for.

We can make our plans, but the LORD *determines our steps* (Prov. 16:9 NLT).

October 3: Giant-Killers

There are no easy answers, but there are simple answers.
We must have the courage to do what we know is morally right.
—Ronald Reagan

David was the first to kill a 10-foot giant Philistine named Goliath in battle. Little did David know that he would inspire a new generation of giant killers after him. Years later, David's servants fought and killed the relatives of Goliath to lead Israel to victory over the Philistines (2 Sam. 21). Had David never become a giant killer, his servants would never have become giant killers either. Likewise, standing up for what is right may feel like a lonely endeavor, but when we do so anyway, in spite of the odds against us, we may be inspiring those after us to join the fight. Let us pray today that we will have the courage of our convictions, doing exactly what God has called us to do so we inspire this courage in others.

If God is for us, who can ever be against us? (Rom. 8:31 NLT).

October 4: Living for a Purpose

> *The mystery of human existence lies not in just staying alive,*
> *but in finding something to live for.*
> —Fyodor Dostoyevsky

People who live their lives for a purpose do not just let life happen to them; they make life happen. Every day of the 33 years Jesus walked on this earth and since the beginning of time, He knew exactly what He was here to do: to die on the cross for the sins of the world. I also have a purpose for writing this book: to encourage people to pursue God's greater purpose for their lives. So that leads me to a very important question. What is your purpose? If you are not sure right now, then take some time to sit down and pray about it and think it through, write it out—and even consider printing it out to hang it up somewhere that you can see it every day. Living out God's greater purpose for your life means that He will do greater things in your life than you would have ever thought possible.

Many are the plans in the mind of a man, but it is the purpose of the Lord that will stand (Prov. 19:21 ESV).

October 5: Bearing Our Burdens

> *As long as a man is alive and out of hell,*
> *he cannot have any cause to complain.*
> —Charles Spurgeon

We tend to think that complaining to our friends and family about our burdens is in some way cathartic and helpful, but often it only makes burdens feel heavier. What if instead of complaining, we simply prayed? If we go to God first with our burdens, He can change how we think and talk about our burdens. Perhaps we will recognize that our burdens are not actually as heavy as we thought. And even if God does not remove the burden from us immediately or ever, for that matter, He can give us new strength to bear our burdens with ease.

Come to me, all you who are weary and burdened, and I will give you rest (Matt. 11:28).

October 6: Questions in Difficult Seasons

*If you don't like something change it; if you can't change it,
change the way you think about it.*
—Mary Engelbreit

Often when people go through difficult seasons of life, they ask God serious questions such as, "Why?" as in "Why would a good God allow this to happen to me?" Scripture says, "He causes his sun to rise on the evil and the good, and sends rain on the righteous and the unrighteous" (Matt. 5:45). Perhaps God would prefer that we ask another set of questions when we go through difficult seasons. Although we cannot always understand why, we can always ask, "What?" as in "God, what do you want to teach me in this season?" Perhaps we learn that God is teaching us to persevere, stay in peace, and maintain noble character in spite of the adversity we are presently going through. You can also ask yourself, "How?" as in "How am I going to respond to adversity?" Ideally, we should always respond in a way that glorifies God and points others to Him. Pray today that you will glorify God in each season of life you go through so He can mold and shape you into the person He is calling you to be.

The LORD is a stronghold for the oppressed, a stronghold in times of trouble (Ps. 9:9 ESV).

October 7: Roller-Coaster-Ridin' Nana

They do not love that do not show their love.
—William Shakespeare

Growing up in the '90s, my grandmother, Nana, would take her grandkids—my sisters Nina and Lindsey; my cousins Auston, Kristen, and Brandon; and I—to a Houston amusement park called Six Flags AstroWorld. Amazingly, a woman in her 60s rode all the rides with her grandchildren, even upside-down rides. And that is why we all started calling her Super Nana. Looking back on those experiences, I don't think Nana enjoyed the rides as much as she enjoyed spending time with her grandchildren and sharing in the activities we enjoyed. This is how she chose to show us her love, and she also created amazing memories in our little minds that we will never forget. Sometimes, it is not enough to just say, "I love you." We need to show our love by sharing activities with the people we love. Let us pray today that we will look for ways to show our love and create memories with those we love.

Let's not merely say that we love each other; let us show the truth by our actions (1 John 3:18 NLT).

October 8: Leaving Weight behind Lesson

Don't dwell on what went wrong. Instead, focus on what to do next.
—Denise Waitley

As I got ready to attend grad school at Liberty University, I packed everything I thought I would need for the semester—in five suitcases. When I arrived at the airport, however, I was informed that I would have to take some weight out of my bags or be forced to pay a hefty fine. Since I was a student on a tight budget, I quickly removed some nonessential items so I could fly without paying the fine. Likewise, when you want to move forward in life, there are some things—negative people, destructive habits, poor mentalities, sin—you cannot take with you if you want to get to your destination. You will have to take an inventory of what you actually need and leave some things behind. Pray today that you will be honest with yourself about the things in your life that are best left behind.

Let us throw off everything that hinders and the sin that so easily entangles (Heb. 12:1).

October 9: Vision Beyond

The only limits are, as always, those of vision.

—James Broughton

Abram lived on his father's land and would presumably inherit it when his father died. Abram's father's land was familiar and comfortable, but God wanted to take Abram to a place that was unknown to him and outside his comfort zone. Abram had never seen this land and did not know which direction to head, but God opened the eyes of Abram's heart to see His vision. In summary, he had vision beyond his comfort zone and beyond what he could see. Here are two lessons for us. First, too often we settle for something familiar and comfortable, but, like Abram, sometimes we have to be willing to set out into the unknown and outside our comfort zones if we are going to pursue the greater life to which God beckons us. Second, we must have vision beyond what we can physically see, trusting God to lead us every step of the way by His Spirit as we pursue the "land" where He has calls us.

Now faith is the assurance of things hoped for, the conviction of things not seen (Heb. 11:1 ESV).

October 10: **Name Change**

Experience is simply the name we give our mistakes.
—Oscar Wilde

God had promised Abram and Sarai a child when Abram was 75. But when Abram was 99, it had not happened yet. Twenty-four years is a very long time to wait for a promise. One day, however, God appeared to Abram and changed his name from Abram to Abraham, which means father of a multitude. He changed Sarai's name to Sarah, which means mother of nations. That is important because before God would perform a miracle, He had to change the way Abraham and Sarah understood and called themselves. Before they had any children, they had to walk around the house calling one another the father of many and the mother of nations. What a faith builder! Some of us would benefit from renaming ourselves and our circumstances. Instead of calling yourself Broken, start calling yourself Blessed. Go from Weak to Strong and from Anxious to Peaceful, from Poor to Favored, and from Miserable to Miracle. This tweak in what you call yourself is not just a matter of changing your mentality from negative to positive, but it is also your expectation that an almighty God can do anything if you simply have faith to trust Him. Give yourself a name change, and trust God to do the miraculous in and through you.

Now to him who is able to do immeasurably more than all we ask or imagine, according to his power that is at work within us (Eph. 3:20).

October 11: Holy Spirit Synergy

Problems can become opportunities when the right people come together.
—Robert South

It is a great feeling to be with people who uplift, energize, and inspire you. When you are with the right people, your creative juices begin to flow, and together you start to have new, exciting, and hopeful thoughts. I like to call this Holy Spirit synergy. Independently, you may not have this kind of experience, but when two or three of you are part of the same team, there is an energy you share that is greater than if you were alone. You see, Jesus spoke to multitudes, but His team was comprised of just 12 men with whom He felt a synergy. He believed they could change the world. In much the same way, we must surround ourselves with people who together create synergy and change. Without other people, we may do some good things, but when we join together as part of a team, the Holy Spirit synergy will enable you to do greater things than you ever could have done alone.

For where two or three have gathered together in My name, I am there in their midst (Matt. 18:20 NASB).

October 12: Strength Training and Goal Setting

Disturb us, Lord . . . when our dreams have come true,
because we have dreamed too little.
—Sir Frances Drake

At the age of 25, after months of striving to get stronger and working through plateaus, I finally bench-pressed 315 pounds (three 45-pound plates on each side of the bar), a milestone in a weight lifter's world. I was so proud of myself. As soon as I accomplished this, I asked myself, "What's next?" I could spend the rest of my days working out, going through the motions to reach an inevitable loss in strength as I aged, or

I could set another goal and keep striving to be better. So I set another strength goal and achieved it. Whether it's strength training goals or any other goals that we set, whenever we reach our goals, let us not be satisfied for too long. May we set new goals to reach our personal best. We are probably all capable of a lot more than we realize, so let us dream bigger. When you achieve your goals, prayerfully ask God to bless you and enlarge your territory so you will achieve all He has called you to be in and through Him.

I can do all things through Christ who strengthens me (Phil. 4:13 NKJV).

October 13: **WrestleMania 2000 and Its Waiting Lesson**

Maybe your deadline doesn't fit God's timeline.
—Mark Batterson

At the age of 12, in the days leading up to Christmas, I ripped the wrapping paper off the top corners of almost every present under the tree. I was looking for WrestleMania 2000 for Nintendo 64. When I found it, I ripped open the package and played the video game until Christmas Eve when I rewrapped it and stuck it back under the tree. My parents never had a clue—how crafty of me! The truth is, I never enjoyed playing that video game as much as I thought I would because I felt such a sense of guilt. I watched my sisters open their gifts at the right time in pure suspense and surprise. I learned a valuable lesson that Christmas: The joy of suspense and surprise when you wait for a good gift is well worth the wait. If you are waiting for God to answer a prayer, there are times the wait may feel excruciatingly difficult. But forcing something to be done our way is never the answer. While we wait for God, may we pray today that He will renew our strength (Isa. 40:31). Maybe we will start to recognize that there are lessons God wants to teach us and character He wants to build in us while we wait. Instead of praying for a good gift ASAP (as soon as possible), let's pray for one ALAT (as long as it takes).

Say, "God, take as long as it takes to accomplish whatever You want to do in me so Your will can be accomplished through me."

The LORD is good to those who wait for him (Lam. 3:25 ESV).

October 14: Undercover Boss

All the world is full of suffering. It is also full of overcoming.
—Helen Keller

In the TV show *Undercover Boss*, a company's CEO goes undercover to work as one of his own employees. By becoming one of them, he can experience the same difficulties, conflicts, and monotony that they experience. At the end of each show, he rewards those who work well with others and do good, honest work even when their boss is not around. God, as all-powerful and all-knowing as He is, manifested Himself in the flesh as Jesus Christ to experience the same sufferings we do. Jesus experienced loneliness, betrayal, hunger, physical pain, loss of a loved one, anger, and many other emotions. Jesus suffered as we suffer, and worse, He was beaten and tortured to die a bloody death on a cross for the sins of the world. Whenever we experience hardships of any kind, let us take comfort in remembering that Jesus has also experienced these sufferings and has overcome them all. If you believe in Jesus, He is in you, and in that way, you can overcome, too. Pray today that Jesus will give you a longsuffering ability to withstand any trial.

Yet what we suffer now is nothing compared to the glory he will reveal to us later (Rom. 8:18 NLT).

October 15: Refresh Others

A kind gesture can reach a wound that only compassion can heal.
—Steve Maraboli

Scripture shows that every encounter with Jesus left others feeling refreshed. It is no wonder He is referred to as "living water." As a result, the masses flocked to Him. In the same manner, may we also leave others feeling refreshed and saying to themselves, "I always feel so good after being around them." Enjoy laughs together, genuinely be interested in them, rejoice and weep with them, encourage them, and simply keep smiling. When you refresh others, then God will refresh you.

Whoever refreshes others will be refreshed (Prov. 11:25).

October 16: Conqueror

Go forth a conqueror and win great victories.
—Virgil

Moses passed away, and God called Joshua to lead Israel to embark on new territory. Moses was the leader Israel respected, so Joshua must have asked himself, "Will anyone follow me?" or "Do I have what it takes?" God responded, "Be strong and courageous. Do not be afraid; do not be discouraged, for the LORD your God will be with you wherever you go" (Josh. 1:9). Joshua became a conqueror. Likewise, you may have your moments where you wonder, "Will they like me?" or "Can I do this?" What God said to Joshua is true for you and for me: "Be strong and courageous" because in Christ we are more than conquerors. God is with you today and every day. The victory is yours.

Overwhelming victory is ours through Christ, who loved us (Rom. 8:37 NLT).

October 17: **Make Room**

There is always room at the top.

—Daniel Webster

The prophet Elisha often ate and visited with a woman and her husband whenever he passed by their home in his travels. Then, they decided to build a room on top of their house so Elisha could stay there from time to time (2 Kings 4). The woman had been barren for many years, and as God would have it, the prophet Elisha let her know that she would have the son she always wanted. God did as Elisha had prophesied. Had the woman and her husband not invited the prophet into their home, they would not have received their blessing from God. It is not always easy to make room for God's will, and it usually costs us something. But when we obey God, then in one way or another, He will bless us. Let us pray today that we will make room for God in our lives.

I will pour out a blessing so great you won't have enough room to take it in! Try it! Put me to the test! (Mal. 3:10 NLT).

October 18: **Quiet Time**

Thou hast created us for Thyself, and our heart is not quiet until it rests in Thee.

—Saint Augustine

Start your day with a quiet time, praying to God and meditating on His promises. It does not have to be long. Simply find a place of peace and rest for your soul, and spend 10 to 15 minutes there. Here are the core elements of prayer: Praise God for who He is. Apologize for sin. Thank Him for what you have. Ask Him for what you need. Just a little time with Him this morning will radically change your paradigm today.

The Lord is near to all who call on him (Ps. 145:18 ESV).

October 19: **Smile**

Always keep your smile. That's how I explain my long life.
—Jeanne Calment

While many of my friends got their braces off in high school, I was just getting mine on when I started my freshman year of college. The idea of what people thought of me made me so insecure that I wouldn't smile for pictures. I thought I'd be called "brace face." When I met new people and greeted them, I usually wouldn't smile because I was embarrassed by the braces. But the reality was that most people were not paying as much attention to my mouth as I was. And even if they did notice my braces, I had no reason to be embarrassed. Even without braces, there will always be reasons not to smile, but there are hundreds if not thousands of reasons to smile. For whatever reason, we can become so engrossed in our problems that we miss out on life's moments to smile. So smile, and do not stop. Just as God smiles down on us in moments that we bring Him joy, we, too, should look every day for moments that fill our lives with hope and joy and that cause us to smile.

GOD bless you and keep you, GOD smile on you and gift you, GOD look you full in the face and make you prosper (Num. 6:24–26 MSG).

October 20: **With Us, in Us**

Let us diligently apply the means, never doubting that a just God, in his own good time, will give us the rightful result.
—Abraham Lincoln

One name for Jesus is Emmanuel, which means "God with us." When Jesus told His disciples that He would be going to the Father, the disciples wondered how Jesus could abandon them. They wanted Jesus with them. Jesus explained that it was better that he left because an advocate, the Holy Spirit, would soon be in them. Jesus explained, "I will come to you"

(John 14:18) through the Holy Spirit. Thus, Jesus went from being God with us to God in us. We may have moments that we do not feel as if God is with us, but remember that God dwells in the heart of every believer. God is not just with us; He is also in us.

Christ in you, the hope of glory (Col. 1:27 ESV).

October 21: Learning from Others

*A wise man can learn more from a foolish question than
a fool can learn from a wise answer.*
—Bruce Lee

No matter what age you are, you will need wise leaders to learn from in order to grow into the leader God has called you to be. I have learned from many leaders, seminars, and books, but the leaders I have learned the most from are my dad, my friend Chet, and my other friend Rafael who is like a second father to me. I am so grateful for the wisdom I have extracted from them and for their prayers that have provided a spiritual covering over my life. I still feel like there is much I need to learn from them. To grow into the leaders God has called us to be and accomplish the assignment He has called us to undertake, we must make ourselves available to learn from leaders He puts in our lives. If you do not have anyone in your life who can mentor you, ask God to give you leaders who will help you grow wiser, trust in Him, and mold you into the leader He has called you to be.

Let the wise hear and increase in learning, and the one who understands obtain guidance (Prov. 1:5 ESV).

October 22: **Being a Friend**

If you go looking for a friend, you're going to find they're very scarce.
If you go out to be a friend, you'll find them everywhere.
—Zig Ziglar

If anyone modeled what it meant to be a friend, it was Jesus. He was a friend to people who were ostracized by society. Jesus took relational risks by continually giving more than He could ever get back. Jesus made Himself available to people and showed Himself friendly, and as a result, many people heard the good news and became friends of God. Perhaps we should consider being a friend to someone shunned by society. Maybe we should take a few relational risks by giving more and expecting nothing in return. And of course, we must also make ourselves available to others and show ourselves friendly. When we look to be a friend to others, God will fill our lives with friendships, and more importantly, we will have opportunities to share the good news with them so they, too, can become friends of God.

A man who has friends must himself be friendly (Prov. 18:24 NKJV).

October 23: **Do Little Things**

There are many of us that are willing to do great things for the Lord,
but few of us are willing to do little things.
—Dwight L. Moody

We often look at biblical characters such as Moses who parted the Red Sea, and we say, "I wish I could do something like that." In our own ways, we all like the idea of doing something great for God. The problem is that if some people do not feel they can do a great thing, then they do nothing. What if this Christian life is more about the little things we are willing to do for God? Perhaps God wants you to help people who are hurting, give generously to the poor, or live a life of purity. Do not discount the little things, because one day, we may discover that the little things were actually the great things.

If you are faithful in little things, you will be faithful in large ones. But if you are dishonest in little things, you won't be honest with greater responsibilities (Luke 16:10 NLT).

October 24: **Leaving the Old Behind**

There are far, far better things ahead than any we leave behind.
—C. S. Lewis

We cannot grab hold of something new if we are still clutching onto something old. It is hard to have new thoughts if our minds are consumed with memories of the past. We often cannot enjoy new relationships if we are still hung up on people who have hurt us. We cannot start and grow successful in new ventures if we are still stuck on failed endeavors. We have to commit to leaving some thoughts, people, and situations behind if we are going to move forward. So let us leave the old behind so we can move forward from here on.

Forget what happened in the past, and do not dwell on events from long ago (Isa. 43:18 GW).

October 25: **Playing the Background**

You take the leading role, and I'll play the background.
—Lecrae

Deborah was the first and only female judge of Israel (the Margaret Thatcher of biblical times). She was a counselor, a warrior, a prophetess, and the wife of Lapidoth. It has been said that behind every good man is a strong woman, but in this scenario, behind the woman was a strong man.

Judges 4:4 is the only mention of Lapidoth. We can assume that Lapidoth recognized and valued that God was tremendously using his wife, so he played the background while she took the leading role. Consequently, Deborah led Israel to victory over their enemies. Make no mistake, this victory was just as much Lapidoth's as it was Deborah's because he supported her through the good times and the bad. Here is my point. We each must play the background so Christ can have the spotlight. If we play by God's script, glorifying Him, we will always win. God will pour out His favor on us and fill our lives with immeasurable blessings.

Come, let us tell of the LORD's greatness; let us exalt his name together (Ps. 34:3 NLT).

October 26: Unfailing Faith

The Christian life is not a constant high. I have my moments of deep discouragement. I have to go to God in prayer with tears in my eyes, and say, "O God, forgive me," or "Help me."
—Billy Graham

Peter did not know he would deny Christ, but Christ knew. Christ exhorted Peter just before it happened by saying, "I have prayed for you, Simon [Peter] that your faith may not fail. And when you have turned back, strengthen your brothers" (Luke 22:32). Peter may stumble, but he would not fail. Even when Peter was about to make a mistake that grieved Christ, Peter's mistake would be forgiven, and Peter would still be used to strengthen his brothers. What a merciful God! You see, strengthening people is what Peter was created to do; that was his gift. After Peter denied Christ, He would later go on to preach on the day of Pentecost and build churches throughout the world. You may have made some mistakes, but realize that all you have to do is apologize to God, ask His forgiveness, and ask for His help to be better. Just as God still used Peter, He will use you and your gifts to fulfill His will.

For God is working in you, giving you the desire and the power to do what pleases him (Phil. 2:13 NLT).

October 27: Do Right Things

> *Managers do things right, but leaders do right things.*
> —Stephen R. Covey

Gideon was the fifth judge of Israel and a valiant military leader who led Israel to victories over their enemies. When the people of Israel invited Gideon to be their king, he declined their invitation (Judges 8:23). Let us pause here and ask ourselves an honest question. What person in their right mind would turn down an opportunity to be king? While Gideon knew it would be a good opportunity for someone, he did not feel it was right for him. Likewise, all the good opportunities that come our way are not necessarily the right opportunities. There are many people who may want you to live out their script for your life, but, like Gideon, you must stay true to the assignment God has called you to do. When you do, rest assured that you will live a more peaceful, fulfilled, and victorious life. Pray today that you will be led by the Spirit to know which opportunities to take and which ones to turn down.

Remember, it is sin to know what you ought to do and then not do it (James 4:17 NLT).

October 28: Encourage Others

> *Everyone has inside of him a piece of good news.*
> —Anne Frank

Speak words of encouragement to others regardless of whether they look like they need it. You really will not know the profound impact it will have on them unless they tell you what they are going through. They may be smiling and appear to have a ton of friends on social media, but on the inside, they may be depressed and have never felt more alone. They may look like they have it all together, but in actuality, their lives may be falling apart. Things are not always as they seem. Ask God in prayer today to give you a discernment to recognize hurting people so you can lift them up. When we faithfully encourage others, God may eventually give us a moment to share the good news with them so they can come to a saving faith in Christ. And even if they are already Christians, they still need encouragement. As we keep pouring ourselves into encouraging others, God will continually fill us up.

So encourage each other and build each other up (1 Thess. 5:11 NLT).

October 29: Making Your Mark

Too many people are dead but just haven't made it official yet.
—John Maxwell

Do not despair on wasted years or because you do not feel you have left a big enough mark on the world. Maybe you cannot affect the entire world, but you can affect your own little part of it. When you throw a stone in the water, there is a ripple effect that often goes further than you realize. Your smile causes others to do the same. Your compliment breeds another compliment. Your gift compels others to give gifts. Your kindness is contagious. Pray today that you would continue to look for ways to do good in the world. Just as Christ took a boy's five loaves and two fishes and multiplied them to feed thousands, He can take the good you do and use it to affect more people than you would have ever thought possible.

Do not neglect to do good and to share what you have, for such sacrifices are pleasing to God (Heb. 13:16 ESV).

October 30: **Mentoring Others**

A mentor is someone who allows you to see the hope inside yourself.
—Oprah Winfrey

In 2008, I took a college summer course taught by a professor whose name was Abby. She had a great impact on me. Not only did I learn from her each day, but she also encouraged me to believe in myself and my academic abilities. If I made a B or a C on a paper, she spent extra time to let me rewrite the paper until I got it right and earned an A. She did not get paid more to mentor me, but she simply went the extra mile out of the goodness of her heart. She wrote a letter of recommendation for me, and I thanked her for all her help. She told me that one day I would pay it forward. I went on to earn my undergraduate and master's degrees and then became a college instructor in communications, just like Abby. Years later, I guest lectured for Abby in her communications class. It was so much fun to honor her by sharing with Abby's class what a godsend she had been to me. Look for ways to give people hope by helping them believe in themselves, just like Abby did for me. Look for people you can become a mentor to so that through you, others can become the very best versions of themselves and reach their fullest potential. Also look for people who can be this for you.

Listen to advice and accept instruction, that you may gain wisdom in the future (Prov. 19:20 ESV).

October 31: **Connecting Flights**

God lets everything happen for a reason. It's all a learning process, and you have to go from one level to another.
—Mike Tyson

While I was in graduate school at Liberty University in Lynchburg, Virginia, direct flights from Houston to Lynchburg simply did not exist.

I had to take a connecting flight through the hub airport in Charlotte, North Carolina, before I could reach Lynchburg. Likewise, there are some places we may want to go in life that we cannot reach without first going through a hub somewhere. Whether it is growing personally, professionally, or in ministry, this is a process that will take time. Sometimes, we must go through the growing pains of maturation, work our way up the corporate ladder, or serve under someone else's vision in order to learn what we must learn to be the leaders God is calling us to be. How well we go through the process will determine how far we ultimately get to go. Let's pray today that we will be willing to wait for God, go through His process, and learn whatever He must teach us. That will help us reach the place where He is calling us and develop into the leaders He desires us to be.

But they who wait for the LORD shall renew their strength; they shall mount up with wings like eagles; they shall run and not be weary (Isa. 40:31 ESV).

November 1: Helping Others

We can't help everyone, but everyone can help someone.
—Ronald Reagan

When the Good Samaritan saw the badly beaten man, he did not say, "I'm praying for you" or "I'm sorry you're going through that." The first and second passersby may have said something like that. Instead, the Good Samaritan decided to do something about the man's pain by taking him to an inn and paying the innkeeper the full cost so the badly beaten man could heal. While the Good Samaritan couldn't do this for everyone, he could do it for someone. And by doing that, he truly made a difference. Likewise, we cannot help everyone, but we can all help someone. So let us prayerfully look for people for whom we can be Christ's hands and feet so we can illuminate Christ to a broken and suffering world.

Carry each other's burdens, and in this way you will fulfill the law of Christ (Gal. 6:2).

November 2: **Being Proactive**

Don't wait for your break. Make your break.
Make it happen for yourself.

—Charlie Day

After finishing most of my graduate work in Virginia, I finished the remaining thesis portion of my degree in Texas while I searched for a job. I did not know where I was going to find a job, but I did know I had a slimmer chance of finding one if I just filled out applications online. I felt that would end up going nowhere. Instead, I volunteered at a political event where I met and briefly spoke with David, who generously passed along my résumé to some of the contacts in his network, and voilà, I had my first campaign job with Greg Abbott when he ran for governor in 2014. To thank David, I took him to lunch, and we formed a friendship. Over the next year, I stayed in touch with David, and later he helped me get my next job with his boss, Senator Ted Cruz, on his 2016 campaign for president. Little did I realize that the two-minute encounter with David would lead me to two vital jobs that launched my career. The lesson I learned is universally true for anyone. You cannot make key contacts from the comfort of your couch. God's word to Abraham was "go, and I will show." You have to be proactive. You have to go out and meet the right people because God's favor always flows through people. Do not idly wait for your break in life; make your break happen for yourself.

Go to the land that I will show you (Gen. 12:1 NLT).

November 3: **Sensing God's Presence**

Always, everywhere God is present, and always He seeks
to discover Himself to each one.

—A. W. Tozer

There are times in our walk with God that we do not feel He is near to us or even hears us. I know I have felt that way at times. Perhaps you long to sense God's presence and hear His voice, but you do not know where to start. Life has been busy, your job is demanding, bills need to be paid, and you do not feel there is time for anything else. I want to encourage you to cut some things out of your schedule—cancel the lunch appointment, wake up earlier, or skip a workout—and make time to connect with God through prayer and His Word. What do you have to lose? When you make time to connect with God every day, your spirit that was numb to Him will awaken, and you will begin sensing His presence again and seeing His hand in everything. God's still, small voice will begin to speak to you in ways you never would have discovered otherwise.

Draw near to God, and He will draw near to you (James 4:8 ESV).

November 4: Stagnancy Is Complacency

> *I always say, complacency is the kiss of death.*
> —Shari Redstone

King David, who had killed the giant Goliath and tens of thousands of Philistines, opted to stay home while his men went to war. During his idle time, he became tempted seeing Bathsheba bathing on her rooftop and fell into adultery with her. To make matters worse, David had Bathsheba's husband slain in battle after he realized Bathsheba was pregnant. Ultimately, his sin cost him and all of Israel. Had David gone into battle with his men, doing what God had called him to do, he never would have gotten himself into this trouble. King David's lesson is also true for us. When we keep ourselves occupied with what God has called us to do, there is little time for things He has not called us to do. We are always doing one of two things. Either we are drawing closer to God and His call on our lives, or we are not. There is no in-between. God asks that we either be hot or cold—but not lukewarm—in our relationships with Him (Rev. 3:16). Stagnancy is complacency because we open ourselves up for the enemy to attack us spiritually. Let us pray today that we will not become stagnant but do everything we can every day of our lives to pursue what God has called us to do.

Do not be overcome by evil, but overcome evil with good (Rom. 12:21 ESV).

November 5: All Is Well

All is well, all is well. Though everything is a mess, all is well.
—Anthony de Mello

There are times in our lives when everything looks like a mess. Maybe we made this mess, or maybe the mess was caused by others. Or maybe it was a little of both. But God has a knack for turning messes into ministries. God turns trials into testimonies. He turns burdens into blessings. Christ is the ultimate comeback king. He was dead on the cross but resurrected and left the grave. No matter how big our messes appear, with God on our side, these messes are not the end. God can turn our situations around in an instant. And even if He chooses not to turn them around right now or ever, we can look back on this moment as time passes to see that God was working in the midst of the mess. We can see that He changed our character to make us more Christlike. And then we can truly believe that all is well.

Let all that I am wait quietly before God, for my hope is in him (Ps. 62:5 NLT).

November 6: **Bye-Bye, Drive-Thru Banking**

Don't mistake activity with achievement.
—John Wooden

I have had some rough times making deposits at the bank. One time, I accidentally left with the drive-thru tube container, and I got all the way home before realizing I had to turn around. Another time, the teller forgot to give back my driver's license before I was well on my way, and I got a call to turn around. Come to find out, I learned I could have been depositing checks using the bank app on my phone! It is so simple. I suspect there are some of us who are trying to be productive doing things we think we have to do, but in reality, we are actually wasting time. Take an inventory of how you spend your time throughout your day, and redeem it doing only what you really need or want to do. By doing so, we will spend our time more wisely and keep ourselves fresh so we have more time for things that matter most.

Look carefully then how you walk, not as unwise but as wise, making the best use of the time (Eph. 5:15–16 ESV).

November 7: **Know Your Identity**

We know what we are, but know not what we may be.
—William Shakespeare

When Jesus fasted in the wilderness, the devil came to tempt Him. The first thing he said to Jesus was, "If you are the Son of God" (Matt. 4:6), as though "if" put it in question. The devil knew who Jesus was, and Jesus did, too, but the devil wanted to see if he could convince Jesus that He was not the Son of God. The devil also likes to question us about our identity and our integrity, especially after we stumble. He wants you to believe that you are not actually a child of God but, instead, a fraud. He knows that if he succeeds, he can lower your confidence so you have less of an impact as a parent, a spouse, a student, an employee, or a leader. Do not fall for it. Know who you are—a child of the most high God. Thus, you have inherited all the power, authority, and confidence that come with being His child.

The thief comes only to steal and kill and destroy. I came that they may have life, and have it abundantly (John 10:10 NRSV).

November 8: Moose Shirts

I've never been a conceited person or cocky, never felt boastful, but I always had a sense of self-worth; I always had a real sense of myself.
—Will Ferrell

In sixth grade, I was determined to be cool enough to sit at the cool kids' lunch table. To do so, I would need help from a very special moose stitched on those faded, too-tight T-shirts made by Abercrombie & Fitch. I scraped together every penny I could and bought expensive moose shirts. The problem was that I only had seven days' worth of moose coolness, and on the eighth day, I would turn back into a loser. "Mom, can you stitch a moose on my other shirts?" Sixth grade was a rough year because I could never get enough of that moose! While Abercrombie & Fitch may no longer be the style, the lesson still applies to you and me since too often we base our self-worth on what is on us rather than what is in us. Maybe you feel like you need to drive a particular brand of car or that your house has to be so many square feet in a certain neighborhood. Or maybe your kids have to be in a fancy private school, and thus the moose can poke out its ugly head in any shape or fashion. Even in times that you do not feel like you have enough or that you are enough, in Christ, you have everything you need, and He is enough.

Keep your lives free from the love of money and be content with what you have (Heb. 13:5).

November 9: **Ask for Wisdom**

Thinking well to be wise: planning well, wiser:
doing well wisest and best of all.

—Malcolm Forbes

God appeared to King Solomon in a dream and asked him what he wanted. Solomon told God he wanted wisdom to lead Israel. God responded that Solomon could have asked for riches and fame, but because he asked for wisdom, He would give it to him along with riches and fame. God could see Solomon's heart was right because he sincerely wanted nothing but to be a wise leader who would make God proud. Whether you are a student or an athlete, whether you manage employees or are a parent to your children, you are a leader in need of wisdom. Ask God to make you wiser, and watch as God gives you all you need and more.

If you need wisdom, ask our generous God, and he will give it to you (James 1:5 NLT).

November 10: **The Real Slim Shady**

Life every man holds dear; but the dear man holds honor far more
precious dear than life.

—William Shakespeare

It was 2002, and my parents said that because my body is the temple of the Holy Spirit, I could not get my ear pierced. I may have heard them, but I chose not to listen. I smuggled myself to the mall to pierce my left ear, which was the style back then as opposed to getting both ears pierced. I inserted a fake diamond into my ear and felt like Eminem's "Real Slim Shady." Later, I was homeless for exactly the eight hours I left that earring in. These days my parents probably wouldn't have as hard of a time with an earring like they did back then, but the underlying lesson I learned is that I must honor the authority God has placed in my life regardless of whether

I agree with them or not. Likewise, there may be some things you may not agree about with your spouse, but you go along with them anyway to keep the peace between you. While your boss may frustrate you to no end, you conduct yourself in a way that honors your boss and keeps the peace. Let us pray today that we will do what we know we must do to honor the important people in our lives.

Haughtiness goes before destruction; humility precedes honor (Prov. 18:12 NLT).

November 11: Ready, Set, Go

Go, send, or disobey.

—John Piper

God sent Ananias to the most unlikely person: Saul of Tarsus (the same Saul who was a Pharisee of Pharisees and persecuted Christians). Ananias could have said, "Nope, I won't go," and history may have looked very different. Saul may not have become Paul. He may not have gone on to write two-thirds of the New Testament and spread the gospel across the world. This all started because Ananias didn't let fear stop him from approaching someone. God wants us to be just as bold about approaching others with the gospel. Like Ananias, your obedience will have ripple effects on not just one person but also on many others. Let us pray today that we will be obedient to God and not be afraid to share the gospel with others. Ready, set, go.

Go into all the world and preach the Good News to everyone (Mark 16:15 NLT).

November 12: **Long Obedience**

Life is a long obedience in the same direction.
—Frederich Nietzche

Life is a long road of obedience in the same direction because you must make decisions every day (without getting sidetracked) that help you reach a destination. You will not just wake up one day later on in life to become the spouse, employee, or parent that you desire to be. If you wish to be a godly future husband or wife, be a godly single man or woman right now while you wait for God to put the right mate in your life. If you want to be an honest employer one day, be an honest employee now. If you desire to be a mother or father who leaves a legacy, then begin spending time with your kids now. Let us pray that we will live our lives with long obedience, today and each day of our lives, to be the person God has called us to be and reach the places He has called us to go.

Let us also lay aside every weight, and sin which clings so closely, and let us run with endurance the race that is set before us (Heb. 12:1 ESV).

November 13: **Pound the Ground**

Pound the rock.
—Tim Duncan

The bedridden prophet Elisha called on King Jehoash to take a bow and shoot an arrow out the window (2 Kings 13). Jehoash shot, and Elisha said he'd have victory over his enemy. Next, Elisha told the king to take arrows and pound the ground. King Jehoash pounded the ground only three times, and then Elisha said he would only be victorious against Israel's enemies three times. He explained that had the king pounded the ground five times, he would have won a total victory over his enemy. It would be easy to think that Elisha was too harsh on the king, but Elisha saw that King Jehoash lacked faith to persevere. The lesson Jehoash learned is also true for us. The difference between victory and defeat is often just a little more faith. Let's pray that today we will have the resilience to keep pounding the ground in faith.

For we walk by faith, not by sight (2 Cor. 5:7 ESV).

November 14: Vision Casting

The only thing worse than being blind is having sight but no vision.
—Helen Keller

To date, I am in my sixth year teaching public speaking online for a local college. One of the assignments I require of my students is a vision-casting speech in which they create personal mission statements, five-year plans, and bucket lists. To my surprise, many of my students have never articulated what they want to accomplish with their lives. After they spend time self-reflecting and writing down their ideas, they enthusiastically present their speeches to their families and friends. One thing they find is that when they cast their visions to their families, it is very validating for them, and then their families and friends often encourage them to carry out their visions. Likewise, if you have no vision for where you are going, then you are probably not going to like where you end up in life. Continue asking God for a clear vision for where you want to go, and have the courage to take the first step in seeing this vision to fruition. Also, have the courage to cast your vision to your trusted friends and family so they can encourage you in carrying out that vision.

Where there is no vision, the people perish (Prov. 29:18 KJV).

November 15: **Misguided Motivation**

What seems to be generosity is often no more than disguised ambition,
which overlooks a small interest in order to secure a great one.
—Francois de La Rochefoucauld

We can do the right things for the wrong reasons. If we flaunt our giving with our friends to appear generous, inform everyone on social media each time we serve, worship to be seen at church, or revel in the sound of our own voice on stage, then our motivation may be misguided. We probably are not doing these things for God or others so much as for ourselves. God is less interested in our sacrifices than He is in our hearts behind our sacrifices: God wants a humble heart that aims to bring Him glory in everything. God is interested in His own glory, not ours, so may we pray to do all we do with a heart to serve Him.

But when you give to someone in need, don't let your left hand know what your right hand is doing (Matt. 6:3 NLT).

November 16: **Submission**

I don't conquer, I submit.
—Giacomo Casanova

Abraham waited 100 years for his son Isaac. The boy was his pride and joy, a dream child. One day God tested Abraham, telling him to sacrifice Isaac on an altar on a mountain in Moriah. Abraham traveled with Isaac to the mountaintop and tied him up as a sacrifice, but then an angel stopped him. God then provided a ram in the thicket as a substitute for Isaac. Sometimes, God's tests can seem like a full-on assault on our hopes and dreams. It's not God's goal to take anything away from us, but rather He is checking the posture of our hearts to ensure that we are putting nothing before Him. Are you totally submitted to God? Is God number one in your life? Submit your heart to God and put Him first, and you will find that there is no freer or more peaceful way to live.

In all your ways submit to him, and he will make your paths straight (Prov. 3:6).

November 17: **Thorns**

The sharp thorn often produces delicate roses.

—Ovid

Have you ever had a problem that just would not go away? Paul described the thorn in his flesh as a messenger from Satan that tormented him and kept him from becoming proud. The thorn was a weakness that pushed Paul to a greater dependence on Christ. Paul even bragged about his weakness because the end result was strength in Christ. Likewise, we cannot conquer our thorns on our own. If all we needed was more discipline or trying harder, we would already have them defeated. Let us pray that we will lean on Christ so our weaknesses become strengths.

For when I am weak, then I am strong (2 Cor. 12:10).

November 18: **Tell the Truth**

Truth is like the sun. You can shut it out for a time,
but it ain't goin' away.

—Elvis Presley

King Ahab of Israel had 400 false prophets tell him that he would win in battle. But before King Jehoshaphat of Judah would align himself with Israel, he said, "Let's find out what the Lord says" (2 Chron. 18:4). The prophet Micaiah was called upon and told to agree that the king would have victory. Micaiah said, "I can tell him only what my God says" (2 Chron. 18:13). Micaiah prophesied that the king would die and Israel would lose. Though Micaiah was imprisoned for speaking the truth, his prophecy proved to be correct, and for him, there was no greater freedom than telling the truth. In our part of the world, few of us will be persecuted for telling the truth, but there may come a time when that is no longer the case. God needs a new generation of truth-tellers who are willing to risk everything for the sake of the gospel. Boldly tell others what God's Word says, and preach the whole counsel of God, leaving nothing out. And through you, God will change the world one person at a time.

And you will know the truth, and the truth will set you free (John 8:32 ESV).

November 19: Peace through the Holy Spirit

God cannot give us a happiness and peace apart from Himself,
because it is not there. There is no such thing.
—C. S. Lewis

Jesus told his disciples that He would soon go to His Father, but He told them not to fret. He would give them a peace of mind and heart that comes with the gift of the Holy Spirit. It is a peace the world cannot give (John 14:27). We can look to find peace in many other places in life such as job security, retirement plans, cars, homes, relationships, and a multitude of other things. While these things are all nice and add value to our lives, they cannot bring us lasting peace that the Holy Spirit can. Ask God in prayer today for this peace through the Holy Spirit, and watch as you tap into something that will surpass your understanding.

And the peace of God, which transcends all understanding, will guard your hearts and your minds in Christ Jesus (Phil. 4:7).

November 20: **Carrying Burdens**

We should try our best to pour out all the burdens in our spirit by prayer until all of them have left us.
—Watchman Nee

For a few years, I routinely picked up my little sister Sophia from her elementary school. She would frequently say that her backpack was too heavy to carry. I would then take it from her and carry it. Likewise, how many people go on and on for months carrying what they were never meant to carry? Perhaps it's guilt, shame, fear, or regret, and before we know it, years go by, and this weight has nearly broken our backs. Jesus put the weight of the world's sin on His shoulders. Whether your load feels light or heavy, you do not have to keep carrying it. Jesus will take your burden from you and give you rest. Just ask.

The LORD helps the fallen and lifts those bent beneath their loads (Ps. 145:14 NLT).

November 21: **God the Redeemer**

Always turn a negative situation into a positive situation.
—Michael Jordan

Samson was Israel's strongest man and greatest warrior. However, he got involved with a woman named Delilah who worked with Israel's enemy, the Philistines. Each day, she pressed Samson for the secret to his strength so she could inform his enemies. While he initially kept the secret to himself, eventually he surrendered and told her that if his hair was cut off, he would lose his strength. While Samson was asleep, Delilah cut his hair. Samson lost his strength, and the enemy easily captured him. The enemy gouged his eyes out, shackled his feet, and forced him to a grind grain in prison. Thankfully, the story did not end there. While Samson was in prison, his hair grew back, and in one last hurrah, he used his strength to bring down the walls of a building and defeat hundreds of his enemies inside. Just as Samson learned, it does not matter how much of a mess we make of our lives because of poor decisions; we are never too far gone that God cannot redeem us. God can turn our messes into miracles for His greater good. Let us pray today that God will begin to use us in spite of the mess we may have made so He is glorified.

And we know that God causes everything to work together for the good of those who love God and are called according to his purpose for them (Rom. 8:28 NLT).

November 22: **Why You Shine**

Don't shine so others can see you. Shine so that through you, others can see Him.

—C. S. Lewis

John the Baptist had a large following of disciples who were very loyal to him. However, when Jesus arrived on the scene, He instantaneously drew attention away from John and onto Himself. Never for one second was John envious of Jesus's fame. He had always known that his job was to prepare the way for Jesus, and he said that he was not even worthy to untie the sandals from Jesus's feet. John touted, "He must become greater; I must become less" (John 3:30). Anything in ministry that does not turn into praise of Jesus turns into pride, so make it your life's mission to bring fame to Jesus's name. What is perhaps more interesting is the way Jesus describes John the Baptist, saying there is nobody on earth greater. The lesson here is simple: When you honor God, He will always honor you.

He must become greater and greater, and I must become less and less (John 3:30 NLT).

November 23: **Be All There**

Wherever you are, be all there.

—Jim Elliot

In the summer of 2014, my buddy Jonathan and I went on a West Coast road trip. Initially, we thought we might fly to the destinations we knew we wanted to see—the Grand Canyon, Yellowstone National Park, and the Redwoods. I'm so glad we drove instead because the places we saw along the way were magnificent. We experienced a scenic sunset on top of a mountain in New Mexico, golden prairies and windmills in Idaho, and a lighthouse on top of a cape in Oregon. In life, sometimes we can be so future-focused on getting to the places we want to go that we miss out on the journey along the way. Let's decide not to get ahead of ourselves, because there is beauty to be seen all around us. Wherever we are, we must be present in the moment to be able to see it.

Make the most of every opportunity (Eph. 5:16 NLT).

November 24: **Doing It for God**

We can do everything through God, but remember that doesn't mean everything at once.

—*Emily of Deep Valley*

Today, if you do not accomplish one more item on your to-do list but spend time in prayer and devotion connecting with your heavenly Father, then you have fulfilled your purpose. Ultimately, it will not be checking off items on your to-do list or having worldly accolades that bring you lasting joy. Connecting to God will be the key to finding His purpose for your life. When you connect with God, even if only for a few minutes, He can begin to speak to you and reroute the course of your day. You will begin to live for a much greater purpose than yourself.

This is the day which the LORD has made; let us rejoice and be glad in it (Ps. 118:24 NASB).

November 25: **Hoping in Christ**

If you have been reduced to God being your only hope,
you are in a good place.

—Jim Laffoon

There are tons of things we could place our hopes in. We could hope in a goal or a dream job, a retirement account or a relationship—and none of these things are bad in and of themselves. But if we are placing our hope in anything but Christ, then we are by definition putting our hope in an idol. You see, an idol doesn't have to be a golden calf. It could be anything that captivates our attention more than God. My point isn't to rebuke us, but simply to ask that we check our hearts today and every day so we put God in His rightful place—first. When we do, God can begin to use us because we start seeing the world through the lens that Christ sees us. And in effect, we become less self-absorbed and more mission-minded, not living for the temporal but for the eternal.

All who have this hope in him purify themselves, just as he is pure (1 John 3:3).

November 26: **Arms Race**

One of the sanest, surest, and most generous joys of life comes from being
happy over the good fortune of others.

—Robert A. Heinlein

In the eighth grade, my best friend Emanuel and I were obsessed with bench pressing. For us, it was the ultimate litmus test of a man's strength. Emanuel was a bit stronger than I was, and that put us (or at least me) in an arm's race to be the best. Usually, I was just five pounds behind him, but as soon as I thought I'd caught up, he'd also get five pounds stronger. One day, Emanuel went for a new bench press record of 200 pounds. While I spotted him and he inched ever closer, I heard my mind scream, "No! No! No! No!" Of course, when he accomplished 200 pounds, what I actually said was, "Good job bro." But I was not really glad for him; I was jealous of him, as if his growing stronger affected whether or not I could also grow stronger! Some people never outgrow a pattern of envy no matter what stage of life they are in. Are you truly glad for your best friend when he or she gets married and you're still single? Or what about when someone younger than you gets the promotion you were vying for? There is nothing wrong with desiring good things. Just don't let desire interfere with your rejoicing in the victories of others. God has enough blessing for all, so trust in His will. Know that God loves you, too, and also wants to bless you.

Be happy with those who are happy, and weep with those who weep (Rom. 12:15 NLT).

November 27: **Be Sanctified**

To progress is always to begin always to begin again.
—Martin Luther

God has called us as Christians out of a lifestyle of sin. We are to go through a process called sanctification, which means we are to become more like Christ every day. Becoming a Christian does not mean we are somehow now perfect without sin, because for as long as we have a pulse, we will wrestle with temptation. But God tasks us with fighting sin by not giving in to temptation, repenting daily, and seeking out accountability so we replace destructive habits with life-giving ones. If you struggle with habitual sin, know that it is never too late to begin anew.

It is God's will that you should be sanctified (1 Thess. 4:3).

November 28: Burdens Are Blessings

Every burden is a blessing.

—Walt Kelly

Moses endured a speech impediment. Jacob walked with a limp. Paul lived with a thorn in his flesh. These burdens may have devastated many other people, but each of these people relied on God for strength, and God used them in a mighty way. Their burdens thus became their blessings. Maybe you deal with a learning disability, crippling anxiety, or chronic depression. When you surrender your burden to God, relying on His strength, He can completely turn your situation around. You will find that your burden is a blessing because God has used you all the more.

For my yoke is easy to bear, and the burden I give you is light (Matt. 11:30 NLT).

November 29: Facing the Fire

There is no success without hardship.

—Sophocles

King Nebuchadnezzar decreed that Babylon must bow to worship the golden idol. Three Jews—Shadrach, Meshach, and Abednego—refused to be bullied into bowing. The king was furious and threatened them with a fiery furnace. The three Jews retorted that their God would rescue them, but even if He did not, they would not bow. They were thrown into the fire, and much to the king's surprise, he saw a fourth person he described as "a son of the gods" (Dan. 3:25). In the midst of the fire, God was with Shadrach, Meshach, and Abednego, just as He is with us through the fires we face. The fire you face may be hot, and the smoke may be thick, but know that God will act as your shield to see you through it. If it is God's will, not a hair on your head will be touched. Pray today to be strengthened by the fires you face and that God will strengthen your resolve and your faith in His salvation.

The LORD your God in your midst, The Mighty One, will save (Zeph. 3:17 NKJV).

November 30: **Without Complaining**

People seem not to see that their opinion of the world is also a confession of their character.
—Ralph Waldo Emerson

Paul wrote the church in Philippi and admonished them by saying, "Do everything without complaining" (Phil. 2:14). Paul knew that when the Philippians complained that things weren't going the way they'd like, they only annoyed the people around them and frustrated themselves. Moreover, guests visiting the church of Philippi would be less likely to befriend anyone and join the church if complaining church folks repelled them. The lesson for Philippi is true for us. People are often attracted to positive people and repelled by negative people. If we want more friends and more people to join our churches, we must resolve to stop complaining about the bad and start praising God for all the good.

Do everything without complaining (Phil. 2:14 NLT).

December 1: **People Who Push You**

I surround myself with good people who make me feel great and give me positive energy.

—Ali Krieger

One of the practices I have initiated with my family—nine of us counting me—is a group text on which we keep one another informed about our lives and encourage each other. There usually isn't a life event that we don't first share with the family before we share it anywhere else. That's how we push each other to keep going. Everyone needs to surround themselves with people who will push them to keep going. It doesn't have to be a family member, but it needs to be someone you can call when you are in a mental rut, someone who can talk some sense into you or uplift you. When you do that, you get closer to fulfilling God's call on your life each day.

One who has unreliable friends soon comes to ruin, but there is a friend who sticks closer than a brother (Prov. 18:24).

December 2: **Fishers of Men**

Chance is always powerful. Let your hook be always cast; in the pool, where you least expect it, there will be a fish.

—Ovid

Peter, a fisherman, had not caught a fish the entire day. Jesus, whom Peter did not yet recognize, approached him on the shore to encourage him to go deeper into the water to cast his nets. Peter took a chance on Jesus, and sure enough, his nets became filled with fish. It could have been all too easy for Peter to talk himself out of taking Jesus up on his offer, because, after all, nobody knew more about fishing than Peter. Little did he know that this one encounter would drastically change the rest of his life. Jesus said, "Follow me, and I will make you become fishers of men"

(Mark 1:17 NASB). God showed that He would provide for Peter, and Peter recognized his true calling was to be a fisher of men instead of a fisherman. The lesson for Peter is also true for us. God will always provide for us, and our true calling is not our occupation but our assignment to be fishers of people to share the gospel with. Then, they can come into a relationship with God. That does not mean we have to quit our jobs to follow Jesus. We follow him to be fishers of people no matter what type of work we do.

Make the most of every opportunity (Eph. 5:16 NLT).

December 3: Being Satisfied

You can never get enough of what you don't need to make you happy.
—Eric Hoffer

King Solomon was the wealthiest man in history. He said, "I denied nothing my eyes desired" (Eccles. 2:10)—designer homes, exquisite foods, exotic concubines, fine wines. Yet at the end of his life, he said these things were "meaningless" (Eccles. 12:8). They were meaningless because he could not take any of them with him after he passed on from this life to the next. We tend to think that more money, more possessions, more influence, or more whatever will make us happy. If what we have right now cannot make us happy, then what makes us think that more of it will make us happy? More of what is meaningless still amounts to meaninglessness. Today, find satisfaction in something that is truly lasting, which is your relationship with Christ. And learn to be content with whatever season of life you are in, with wherever you are, and with whatever you have.

For I have learned how to be content with whatever I have (Phil. 4:11 NLT).

December 4: **Holy Curiosity**

Now that I am a Christian, I do have moods in which the entire thing looks very improbable; but when I was an atheist, I had moods in which Christianity looked terribly probable.

—C. S. Lewis

Being sound Christians does not mean we will never have questions. On the contrary, we may have a lot of questions that don't come with easy answers. A dose of doubt is entirely healthy in our faith journey, because it is the testing of our beliefs against our experiences that makes them deeper and more meaningful. While we may never fully understand God, when we look to the heavens with a holy curiosity, God looks down on us and smiles.

These trials will show that your faith is genuine. It is being tested as fire tests and purifies gold—though your faith is far more precious than mere gold. So when your faith remains strong through many trials, it will bring you much praise and glory and honor on the day when Jesus Christ is revealed to the whole world (1 Pet. 1:7 NLT).

December 5: **Look Up**

Earth has no sorrow that Heaven cannot heal.

—Thomas Moore

One day, Peter and John approached a lame beggar at the Temple gate. Hanging his head and looking down, the man asked Peter and John for money, but Peter told him, "Look at us." Peter explained that they didn't have money, but they did have something invaluable. He declared in the name of Jesus Christ of Nazareth that the man should "get up and walk" (Acts 3:6 NLT). The man got up and walked. Likewise, life happens to us all, and consequently, we sometimes are left with lingering inhibitions, emotional handicaps, or spiritual hang-ups. We need healing from God,

Jehovah Ropha, the only one who can. We must not hang our heads any longer. The first step in allowing God to heal us is to look up.

But you, O LORD, are a shield about me, my glory, and the lifter of my head (Ps. 3:3 ESV).

December 6: Staying in Peace

First keep peace with yourself, then you can bring peace to others.
—Thomas à Kempis

Falsely accused by the Jews and taken prisoner by the Romans, Paul would have to appeal his case to Caesar. That meant he would have to be transferred from Caesarea to Rome by ship. While the ship was sailing, a storm came that greatly distressed the sailors and soldiers on board. Paul, however, stayed in peace. Since Paul was the only Christian on board, he knew to cling closely to Christ amid life's storms, and he thus heard God's voice to encourage his captors, saying, "You're going to come out of this without even a scratch!" (Acts 27:34 MSG). We also go through our own storms in life, and when we do, like Paul, we have to cling closely to Christ so we can know the peace that only He can bring. Moreover, we must ask that God will use us as He did Paul to encourage others in our times of distress so they, too, can know the source of our peace.

And the peace of God, which surpasses all understanding, will guard your hearts and your minds in Christ Jesus (Phil. 4:7 ESV).

December 7: **New Ending**

Though no one can go back and make a brand new start, anyone can start from now and make a brand new ending.

—Card Bard

Samuel anointed Saul king of Israel, but Saul fell out of favor with God after he disobeyed Him. Then, God told Samuel that He had given the kingdom to someone better than Saul. Samuel told Saul what God said, and scripture says Samuel mourned over Saul. While Samuel was first reluctant about appointing Saul king, he believed that God had a plan in choosing Saul. Perhaps Samuel had seen the potential in Saul and imagined all the possibilities of what Saul and Israel could be together. But his high hopes abruptly came to an end. He might have asked God, "So this is your plan?" That is when God asked Samuel, "How long will you mourn for Saul?" (1 Sam. 16:1). In not so many words, God basically told Samuel to move on. God had chosen a better king for Israel, and it was Samuel's duty to find him. Likewise, sometimes we mourn too long over situations when what we really ought to do is just move on. There is nothing wrong with shedding tears since it is a healthy expression of grief. But I would contend that God does not want you to grieve for the rest of your life. Move on to meet new people, go to new places, and try new activities. Just watch as God begins to do something new in you.

For I am about to do something new. See, I have already begun! Do you not see it? I will make a pathway through the wilderness. I will create rivers in the dry wasteland (Isa. 43:19 NLT).

December 8: Man's Approval and God's Favor

It is better to be looked over than overlooked.

—Mae West

God instructed Samuel to go to Jesse's home to anoint the next king of Israel. When Samuel arrived at Jesse's home, Jesse showcased seven of his sons but excluded his youngest, David. It is probable that when Jesse knew Samuel wanted to pick a king from his family, he overlooked David because he did not think David looked like royalty. David's brothers were strapping soldiers, but David was a scrawny shepherd boy. However, Samuel asked, "Are these all the sons you have?" (1 Sam. 16:11 NLT). Jesse called for David, and we can only imagine what David's thoughts were once he realized why Samuel was there. It was probably something like, "Wow! Seriously, Dad?" Samuel sensed the favor of God on David's life and anointed him the next king of Israel. The lesson for David is also true for you and me. Whenever someone does not approve of us, we need to remember that we don't need the approval of people when we have the favor of God. There will always be people in our lives who doubt our potential that God recognizes, but we need to just keep going, knowing that God has a plan for us.

I have placed before you an open door that no one can shut (Rev. 3:8).

December 9: Taking Time

No great thing is created suddenly.

—Epictetus

After Samuel anointed David the next king of Israel, David did not immediately take the throne. It was a process. David worked for Saul, who was his predecessor. Gradually, the shepherd boy turned giant killer and military general increased in favor and popularity with the people of Israel. Recognizing that God's hand was on David's life, Saul persecuted David and forced him to flee. Though David had opportunities to take circumstances into his own hands and kill Saul, David knew this would not speed up the process of his becoming king. On the contrary, it would likely only hurt him politically. David honored the position of authority that God had given Saul, and consequently, in God's perfect timing, He gave the kingdom to David. It's the same for us. Often, the more we try to force circumstances to work out the way we would like, the more we end up frustrated. It is also possible that if we got our way, we would not actually like the end result. It is God, not people, who sets up and tears down kings (Dan. 2:21), so we must remember that He always has a time and a plan. We must trust in God's providence. The sooner we are at peace with God's timing, the better off we will be in fulfilling God's purpose for us every day.

But they that wait upon the LORD shall renew their strength; they shall mount up with wings as eagles; they shall run, and not be weary; and they shall walk, and not faint (Isa. 40:31 KJV).

December 10: A Father's Grace

The difference between mercy and grace? Mercy gave the prodigal son a second chance. Grace gave him a feast.
—Max Lucado

The Prodigal Son squandered his inheritance due to his sin, forfeiting his sonship, and yet his father welcomed him back with open arms with a feast fit only for an heir. This parable serves as an illustration of the grace our Father showed us by giving us His Son Jesus to die on the cross for our sins. We certainly didn't deserve that mercy, but God gave us a second chance. Then, being so rich in grace, our Father, through Jesus's resurrection, made us new creations so we could be His sons and daughters and receive an inheritance. No matter who you are or what you've done, don't let the enemy deceive you into thinking that God isn't good enough to forgive you and make you anew. God infinitely loves us. His grace is not only sufficient, but it is abundantly good.

But by the grace of God I am what I am (1 Cor. 15:10).

December 11: People-Pleasers

You can please some of the people all of the time,
you can please all of the people some of the time,
but you can't please all of the people all of the time.
—Abraham Lincoln

Jesus taught the good news, and while many were greatly blessed by His teaching, the Pharisees were displeased with Him. Jesus, however, refused to back down from His message. Consequently, the Pharisees criticized and crucified Him for it. For Jesus, it was never an option to try to please everyone, because that was impossible. If Jesus had tried to please everyone, He would have done a grave disservice to those He was called to reach, and His message would have been meaningless. For chronic people-pleasers, it is hard to reconcile that it is impossible to please everyone all the time. Eventually, you will have to be okay letting some people go on being displeased with you. Stay true to your values, to the people who really love you, and, above all else, to God. In the end, all that matters will be hearing God say these words: "Well done, good and faithful servant" (Matt. 25:21).

Your approval means nothing to me (John 5:41 NLT).

December 12: Knowing Your Identity

The more we focus on who we are in Christ, the less it matters who we were in the past, or even what happened to us.
—Joyce Meyer

In sixth grade, I felt I was rather chubby. One day I wore a yellow shirt, and as I walked down the hallway, a snotty kid yelled, "Here comes the school bus!" It is funny writing material now, but back then, it hurt. Now I believe my weight was normal, considering my age and height, but that wasn't my belief then. In high school, I began lifting weights to prove I was actually a sleek sports car! By ninth grade, even though my physical appearance had changed because I had some muscles, there were times when I looked in the mirror, and insecurity still had me seeing a chubby sixth grader. No matter what the mirror reflected, it could not change how I felt about myself. What I learned at an early age is still true for us today. It does not matter how much working out we do or what clothes we wear or what our hair looks like, if we do not like who we are on the inside, then nothing on the exterior can fix it. Strip everything on the exterior away, and who are we? We have to find a self-confidence that is so much greater than what we look like, a self-confidence that is rooted in our identity in Christ. We find out who we are when we know whose we are. Our self-confidence must flow from a realization that we do not belong to ourselves and that we are His masterpieces, fearfully and wonderfully made (Ps. 139:14).

This means that anyone who belongs to Christ has become a new person. The old life is gone; a new life has begun! (2 Cor. 5:17 NLT).

December 13: Praying Like Breathing

To be a Christian without prayer is no more possible than to be alive without breathing.
—Martin Luther King, Jr.

What happens when you hold your breath? Your body becomes so low on oxygen that eventually you have no choice but to breathe or suffocate. After neglecting to pray for hours, we become spiritually depleted because prayer functions as the God-breathed oxygen that sustains and strengthens us throughout the day. Keep breathing, and keep praying.

Pray without ceasing (1 Thess. 5:17 ESV).

December 14: **Embracing the Struggle**

If there is no struggle, there is no progress.
—Frederick Douglass

Jacob's name in Hebrew means supplanting. This name was appropriate because he had swindled his older brother Esau out of his birthright and blessing. Jacob was intent on getting a blessing from God his way, but God was determined to bless Jacob in His own way. One night while Jacob was sleeping, an angel of God wrestled with Jacob. After struggling with Jacob until daybreak, the angel told Jacob to let him go. Jacob replied, "Not until you bless me." The angel asked Jacob, "What is your name?" Jacob told him, and then the angel replied, "Your name will no longer be Jacob, but Israel, because you have struggled with God and with humans and have overcome" (Gen. 32:28). In effect, the name change was a character change, and God turned a swindler into a struggler. Israel's lesson is true for us, too. We must hold onto God's promises in faith, because eventually He will bless, and in doing so, God seeks to make our character more like His own.

Rejoice always, pray without ceasing, give thanks in all circumstances; for this is the will of God in Christ Jesus for you (1 Thess. 5:16–18 ESV).

December 15: **Looking Ahead**

It is always wise to look ahead, but difficult to look further than you can see.
—Winston Churchill

God asked Lot to evacuate his family from the city of Sodom and Gomorrah because the city would soon be destroyed. His request also insisted that they not look back or they would be turned into salt. Much to Lot's dismay, his wife looked back. Lot's wife's eyes give us an indication of the condition of her heart. While she may have physically been in a better place, spiritually she was looking back on what she felt she had left behind. Her mind simply couldn't fathom that God had something better prepared for them than what she was leaving behind. If we let God lead our lives, then what is before us is always better than what is behind us. You cannot control every passing mood or thought, but you do not have to dwell there. Keep looking ahead and moving forward. God has better things in store.

Forgetting what is behind and straining toward what is ahead (Phil. 3:13).

December 16: Finding Inspiration

You can't wait for inspiration. You have to go after it with a club.
—Jack London

I've been writing for many years now, and one thing I learned is that I cannot simply wait to be struck with inspiration. Otherwise, I might be looking at a blank sheet of paper for hours. Sometimes, I just write to produce something, and after I write for a while, the words on the paper somehow seem to come together. Here is the point. Do not use a lack of inspiration as an excuse not to do what you say you love. If you're a painter, paint. If you're a dancer, dance. If you're a singer, sing. Get to work, and work hard. Eventually, inspiration will show up.

The hand of the diligent will rule (Prov. 12:24 ESV).

December 17: Taking Rest

He that can take rest is greater than he that can take cities.
—Benjamin Franklin

Jesus's journeys throughout Israel meant He needed rest. As Jesus tried to find a remote place, a huge crowd recognized Him, and He had compassion on them. So, He taught them and performed a miracle to feed them. Afterward, Jesus went away to the mountainside alone to pray. It is obvious that while Jesus loved helping others, He also felt a need to help Himself. Had Jesus not done so, He may not have been as effective in carrying out His mission. For us, there comes a time when the best option for ourselves and others is pressing our pause buttons. We need rest— whether it's spending time in prayer, reading good books, or catching up on sleep—so we can more effectively carry out our missions.

Come to me, all you who are weary and burdened, and I will give you rest (Matt. 11:28).

December 18: Keeping Ourselves Down

As long as you keep a person down, some part of you has to be down there to hold him down, so it means you cannot soar as you otherwise might.
—Marian Anderson

King Saul could see that God's favor was with his employee David. In those days, one became famous for becoming a military success. It was obvious that David had become a national sensation when people sang, "Saul has slain his thousands, and David his tens of thousands" (1 Sam. 18:7). For the rest of Saul's life, he did everything he could to hold David down, withholding what he owed him, manipulating and slandering him, and even trying to kill him. Saul became a shell of the man he once was. It's now time to do some honest soul-searching to ask ourselves this question: Does someone else have to lose in order for us to win? We scheme covertly or overtly to ensure some rival does not get what they want (influence, affection, position). In effect, we become meaner and smaller than our best selves. Most of the time, others see our meanness for what it is, and we lose out on opportunities we may have had. Today, decide to have this mindset: When I help others rise, I will also rise.

Let each of you look not only to his own interests, but also to the interests of others (Phil. 2:4 ESV).

December 19: **Working with Excellence**

Through hard work, perseverance and a faith in God, you can live your dreams.

—Benjamin Carson

Daniel always worked with excellence, but his Jewish customs irritated his prejudiced Babylonian coworkers. They were jealous of Daniel, believing that a Jew had no place in their industry. Consequently, Daniel was slandered, manipulated, used, and betrayed. Worse, Daniel's coworkers schemed against him to have him thrown into a lions' den for exercising his faith, which was something he could not relent on. Yet Daniel maintained that he would do his best and honor God anyway. It is no wonder God delivered Daniel from the lions' den and promoted him. Likewise, we have to work with excellence and honor God in spite of those who are against us. Others may or may not give you recognition for your work or despise you through no fault of your own, but as scripture says, "If God is for us, who can ever be against us?" (Rom. 8:31). Whenever you do your best to glorify God, whether you are promoted right away, later, or never, you fulfill His greater purpose for you each day that you work.

Whatever you do, work heartily, as for the Lord and not for men (Col. 3:23 ESV).

December 20: **Surety**

One word from God can change your life.

—Kenneth Copeland

One day Jesus met a Roman military officer who explained that his servant was sick. Jesus responded by saying, "I will come and heal him" (Matt. 8:7 ESV). The officer replied, "I am not worthy to have you come under my roof, but only say the word, and my servant will be healed"

(Matt. 8:8 ESV). Perhaps without knowing a lot about Jesus's teachings, the officer simply understood that Jesus had authority to radically change his situation. Jesus replied, "With no one in Israel have I found such faith" (Matt. 8:10 ESV). Funny how someone who was not a follower of Jesus could have more faith than those who followed Him. The lesson is that it doesn't matter who you are—whether you follow Jesus or you're far from Him—just one word from Jesus is more than enough to turn your situation around.

You may ask me for anything in my name, and I will do it (John 14:14).

December 21: Hunkyshet

Nothing is ever really lost to us as long as we remember it.
—L. M. Montgomery

One year my family tried Icelandic Hangikjöt, smoked lamb, instead of the usual turkey Christmas entrée. Almost everyone made fun of its name—it didn't sound appetizing because it sounded like an American curse word. Some wanted to go back to turkey, but it was important to my Icelandic mother that we at least try it. We did, and it grew on us. Now, Hangikjöt has been a Christmas tradition for the last decade. Sometimes, the best gifts are not material. For my mom, it was Hangikjöt, and you cannot put a price tag on that. This Christmas, find new ways to make memories by giving in such a way that truly brings people joy. When you do, you will find that God gives you joy.

Do not withhold good from those to whom it is due, when it is in your power to do it (Prov. 3:27 ESV).

December 22: **Killing Sin**

Christians are called to wage war against this enemy, knowing that there are only two options: Be killing sin or it will be killing you.
—John Owen

Most of us would never take on a full-grown roaring lion as a pet. But if we allow just a little sin into our lives, rationalizing that it's not hurting anyone or it's just a white lie, it's like adopting a lion cub. It's so cute and cuddly, and it may seem like we have contained it at first, but in time, that cub will grow into a ferocious animal we can no longer control. Scripture teaches, "Be alert and of sober mind. Your enemy the devil prowls around like a roaring lion looking for someone to devour" (1 Pet. 5:8). The wages of sin are always death. Sin cannot be controlled or contained, so we must kill any sin that will eventually do the same to us.

Put to death, therefore, whatever belongs to your earthly nature: sexual immorality, impurity, lust, evil desires and greed, which is idolatry (Col. 3:5).

December 23: **Do It Your Way**

True happiness involves the full use of one's power and talents.
—John W. Gardner

Shagmar once defeated 600 of Israel's Philistine enemies by himself. If that was not impressive enough, he did not fight with a machine gun or a king's sword; his weapon of choice was a tool he worked with daily: an ax goad (Judges 3:31). That implies that Shagmar was not a typical soldier. He was probably a farmer. Even so, when it came time to fight, he fought heroically with his God-given tool, and he won. Shagmar saved Israel and glorified God. What if Shagmar had chosen a sword instead of an ax goad? He may not have been as effective, and the outcome might have been different. Here is my point. Whether you teach, write, sing, dance, or design websites, you must use your God-given tool to glorify God. If you get sidetracked trying to fight the good fight someone else's way, you will not be as effective, and the outcome may not be what you had hoped for. Stay true to yourself, fight with your tool, and the victory will be yours.

Now it is required that those who have been given a trust must prove faithful (1 Cor. 4:2).

December 24: The Giver Is the Gift

There is a huge and important difference between enjoying a person who gives gifts and enjoying the gifts instead of the person (or more than the person).

—John Piper

Are we desiring God's gifts more than we desire God? I ask this recognizing that God loves to give good gifts to His children and that it isn't wrong for us to ask Him for gifts. However, as long as we are looking for satisfaction in God's gifts, we miss out on finding true satisfaction in the Giver of those gifts. Even if God never gave one thing more, Christ is more than enough. He alone is reason to continue to faithfully serve God. When God chooses to bless us, let us enjoy it, but may our hearts and minds be fixed on treating Christ as the ultimate gift that He is.

Thanks be to God for his inexpressible gift! (2 Cor. 9:15 ESV).

December 25: A Gift-Giver

However many blessings we expect from God, His infinite liberality will always exceed all our wishes and our thoughts.

—John Calvin

Did you know that it is not only okay but pleasing to God for us to ask Him to meet our needs? Our heavenly Father takes delight in blessing His children, just as any good earthly father enjoys blessing his children. Our heavenly Father blesses us because He loves us. Scripture says, "If you, then, though you are evil, know how to give good gifts to your children, how much more will your Father in heaven give good gifts to those who ask him!" (Matt. 7:11). We cannot fathom the infinite goodness of our heavenly Father. It is far greater than we can ever quantify. We can ask our heavenly Father for anything according to His gracious and sovereign will, confident He will always do what is best for us.

Every good thing given and every perfect gift is from above, coming down from the Father of lights, with whom there is no variation or shifting shadow (James 1:17 NASB).

December 26: Waiting for God

You can save a lot of time waiting on God.
—Adrian Rodgers

I have heard that the best things come to those who wait. While that may sound good in theory, it can often be hard to put into practice. It can be exhausting waiting for a dream to come true or for God to answer our prayers because we are used to instantaneous results. If you do not believe me, go through any fast-food drive-thru and wait for more than five minutes to receive your food. A little frustrating, right? It is liberating to recognize that there are opportunities we cannot force open, but rather we have to wait for them to open. You and I cannot make someone fall in love with us or force our bosses to give us raises, and we cannot become overnight successes. These things inevitably take time. I am not suggesting that we do not strive to be all that God has called us to be, but we ought to remember that all the striving in the world won't cause a flower to bloom before its time.

The LORD is good to those who wait for him, to the soul who seeks him (Lam. 3:25 ESV).

December 27: Like Talking to a Friend

Prayer is simply talking to God like a friend and should be the easiest thing we do each day.

—Joyce Meyer

Have you ever had a friend you could tell anything to, and the conversation would always pick up wherever it left off? That is the way God desires to talk with us. Perhaps you already have a quiet time with God in the mornings, and maybe you already pray before you eat your meals or before you go to bed. But there is another level of prayer that God wants you to enter. Paul encourages Christians to "pray without ceasing" (1 Thess. 5:17 NASB). In other words, maybe you are in the car on your way to work and you turn talk radio off so you can talk with God. Or maybe you ask God for wisdom right before an important meeting or for protection before a trip somewhere. Talk with God like a friend, telling Him your concerns, and then pause for a couple of minutes to hear from Him. These types of fluid and ongoing conversations are the raw and real ones God desires to have with us.

Look to the LORD and his strength; seek his face always (1 Chron. 16:11).

December 28: Sojourners for Christ

The fool wanders, a wise man travels.

—Thomas Fuller

God describes the people of Israel as sojourners because they were just passing through the territories they lived in—Egypt, the desert, and Babylon—en route to the Promised Land. We, too, are only passing through this life en route to God's Promised Land—heaven—for every follower of Christ. May we not wander through this life by living as if our career pursuits, retirement plans, and vacation opportunities are all that matter, but may we remember that this life is only temporary. "Your life is like the morning fog—it's here a little while, then it's gone" (James 4:14 NLT). God has called us each to be sojourners—travelers—for a very specific purpose: to bring God glory by knowing Him a little more each day and making Him known everywhere we go.

We are here for only a moment, visitors and strangers in the land as our ancestors were before us. Our days on earth are like a passing shadow, gone so soon without a trace (1 Chron. 29:15 NLT).

December 29: Power in His Name

How sweet the name of Jesus sounds, in a believer's ear! It soothes his sorrows, heals his wounds, and drives away his fear.
—John Newton

Did you know there's power in the name of Jesus? Scripture says that there is healing in His name (Mal. 4:2), that demons tremble at the sound of His name (James 2:19), and that we can ask for anything in His name, and He will do it (John 14:14). We can pray in the name of Jesus, and the chains of sorrow, sin, and addiction can be instantly broken. May we change the way we pray, trusting that there is supernatural power in His name and that He is truly our Savior and deliverer.

Whatever you ask in my name, this I will do, that the Father may be glorified in the Son (John 14:13 ESV).

December 30: Hungering for Righteousness

There are only two kinds of men: the righteous who think they are sinners and the sinners who think they are righteous.
—Blaise Pascal

Sin is usually pleasurable for a season, but the season will inevitably come to an end. What once made us happy will not be accompanied by lasting peace. It is like being extremely hungry and trying to fill ourselves with cake and ice cream; we might be full afterward, but we are not fulfilled. We might even feel sick. "Bread of deceit is sweet to a man; but afterwards his mouth shall be filled with gravel" (Prov. 20:17 KJV). Sin always leaves a bad aftertaste. Eating healthy foods of spiritual righteousness may not taste as sweet at first, but eventually, we will start to yearn for it once we taste and see that it's good for us.

Blessed are those who hunger and thirst for righteousness, for they shall be satisfied (Matt. 5:6 ESV).

December 31: Open Doors

When one door is closed, don't you know, another is open.
—Bob Marley

We usually don't understand why God closes a door. "God, don't you know I would have been perfect for that job?" or "God, I really wanted that person to be the one." I have learned that it is often in hindsight that we see that God had an even greater door in store. It is a couple of applications later that we find the dream job with better benefits. It's a couple months later that we meet the right person. Trust God to open the right doors in His perfect timing, but also ask Him to shut the doors that He would not have you walk through. That way, you are completely submitted to God and His will for your life.

I have set before you an open door, which no one is able to shut (Rev. 3:8 ESV).

CONCLUSION

Now that you have finished this daily devotional book, my prayer for you is that you would keep to a regular practice of carving out time to spend time with God every day in prayer and the Word. Let Jesus begin to speak to your heart and continue to guide your every step. Even in those moments that you grow weary, God will renew you so you can get your second wind to keep going. That really is the key. Just keep going. And when you do, there will be no stopping you.

If you would like to connect with me, feel free to call me anytime at (713) 449-3084. I try to make myself available to talk anytime, but leave a message if I don't answer right away. I'll always do my best to get back to you. May God bless you on your journey.

ACKNOWLEDGMENTS

There are some people I want to thank for helping me complete this book.

I want to thank my parents. They've read nearly every one of my daily devotionals and have given me good feedback. And they have shaped more of my thoughts than I can ever write down. I also want to thank my sisters Nina, Lindsey, Annelissa, and Sophia. My family members have always been my biggest fans.

I also want to thank Rafael Cruz for helping to shape my views on faith and increase my trust in God. Those thousands of hours we spent traveling around the country and working together in multiple capacities have made me a better man.

Although I have only had brief encounters with Pastor Steven Furtick and Pastor Mark Batterson, they have shaped my views on faith perhaps more than any other teachers. I have thoroughly enjoyed reading their books and listening to their sermons.

I have never met Max Lucado, but it was his daily devotional that I got in my email inbox every day many years ago that encouraged me to start writing. He has inspired me in a very big way.

I have only briefly met Bob Goff. After reading his book, I found his phone number at the end and decided to call him. We had a good conversation, and he told me that to be a good writer, I needed to (1) write in the same voice I speak in and (2) take notes on the seemingly monotonous moments in life and write about them. His idea to include his phone number at the end of his book is why I'm listing mine in this book.

I want to thank the great leaders who have offered to lend their names as endorsements. You inspire me more than you know.

I want to thank Congressman Kevin Brady. I appreciate having been given the opportunity to work for a man I greatly admire and respect. He's one of the most principled, hardworking, and goodhearted people I've ever met. He makes it a point to humbly check his ego at the door every day to serve his country and his constituents for the right reasons.

I want to thank my pastor, Jason Shepperd. I thoroughly enjoy getting to be a part of Church Project under his leadership. Each Sunday, the teaching is inspirational, thought-provoking, and convicting…and many times his sermons have inspired many thoughts in me that have come out in my writing.

I want to thank Dawn Allen for following my daily devotional posts online and offering to edit my book. She did a thorough job. And finally, I want to thank the Lucid Books team for helping me put this book together to meet the deadline. You all kept me on track so I could publish this book.

SCRIPTURE INDEX

A

Page 25: *Then the Lord said to him, "Take off the sandals from your feet"* (Acts 7:33 ESV).

Page 6: *A man after my own heart* (Acts 13:22).

Page 125: *And the disciples were filled with joy and with the Holy Spirit* (Acts 13:52 ESV).

C

Pages 33, 139: *Oh, that you would bless me and enlarge my territory!* (1 Chron. 4:10).

Page 160: *O give thanks to the Lord, call on His name; make known His doings among the peoples!* (1 Chron. 16:8 AMPC).

Page 226: *Look to the Lord and his strength; seek his face always* (1 Chron. 16:11).

Page 154: *Give to the LORD the glory he deserves! Bring your offering and come into his presence. Worship the LORD in all his holy splendor* (1 Chron. 16:29 NLT).

Page 227: *We are here for only a moment, visitors and strangers in the land as our ancestors were before us. Our days on earth are like a passing shadow, gone so soon without a trace* (1 Chron. 29:15 NLT).

Page 81: *If my people, who are called by my name, will humble themselves and pray and seek my face and turn from their wicked ways, then I will hear from heaven, and I will forgive their sin and will heal their land* (2 Chron. 7:14).

Page 11: *So that you may live a life worthy of the Lord and please him in every way: bearing fruit in every good work, growing in the knowledge of God* (Col. 1:10).

Page 98: *Christ is the visible image of the invisible God. He existed before anything was created and is supreme over all creation* (Col. 1:15 NLT).

Page 182: *Christ in you, the hope of glory* (Col. 1:27 ESV).

Page 117: *Set your minds on things that are above, not on things that are on earth* (Col. 3:2 ESV).

Page 156: *Think about the things of heaven, not the things of earth* (Col. 3:2 NLT).

Page 59: *Put to death therefore what is earthly in you: sexual immorality, impurity, passion, evil desire, and covetousness, which is idolatry* (Col. 3:5 ESV).

Page 223: *Put to death, therefore, whatever belongs to your earthly nature: sexual immorality, impurity, lust, evil desires and greed, which is idolatry* (Col. 3:5).

Page 160: *Bear with each other and forgive one another if any of you has a grievance against someone. Forgive as the Lord forgave you* (Col. 3:13).

Page 84: *And whatsoever ye do in word or deed, do all in the name of the Lord Jesus, giving thanks to God and the Father by him* (Col. 3:17 KJV).

Page 90: *And whatever you do, whether in word or deed, do it all in the name of the Lord Jesus, giving thanks to God the Father through him* (Col. 3:17).

Page 163: *Let every detail in your lives—words, actions, whatever—be done in the name of the Master, Jesus, thanking God the Father every step of the way* (Col. 3:17 MSG).

Page 118: *Whatever you do, work heartily, as for the Lord and not for men* (Col. 3:23 ESV).

Page 130: *Work willingly at whatever you do, as though you were working for the Lord rather than for people* (Col. 3:23 NLT).

Page 128: *Conduct yourselves with wisdom toward outsiders, making the most of the opportunity. Let your speech always be with grace, as though seasoned with salt, so that you will know how you should respond to each person* (Col. 4:5–6 NASB).

Page 40: *God is faithful, who has called you into fellowship with his Son, Jesus Christ our Lord* (1 Cor. 1:9).

Page 162: *Isn't it obvious that God deliberately chose men and women that the culture overlooks and exploits and abuses, chose these "nobodies" to expose the hollow pretensions of the "somebodies"?* (1 Cor. 1:28–29 MSG).

Page 33: *That your faith might not rest in the wisdom of men but in the power of God* (1 Cor. 2:5 ESV).

Page 27: *So neither the one who plants nor the one who waters is anything, but only God, who makes things grow* (1 Cor. 3:7).

Page 224: *Now it is required that those who have been given a trust must prove faithful* (1 Cor. 4:2).

Page 42: *I am made all things to all men, that I might by all means save some* (1 Cor. 9:22 KJV).

Page 112: *To the weak I became weak, to win the weak. I have become all things to all people so that by all possible means I might save some* (1 Cor. 9:22).

Page 124: *So I run with purpose in every step* (1 Cor. 9:26 NLT).

Page 215: *But by the grace of God I am what I am* (1 Cor. 15:10).

Page 126: *Do not be misled: "Bad company corrupts good character"* (1 Cor. 15:33).

Page 95: *Let all that you do be done in love* (1 Cor. 16:14 ESV).

Page 70: *He comforts us in all our troubles so that we can comfort others. When they are troubled, we will be able to give them the same comfort God has given us* (2 Cor. 1:4 NLT).

Page 127: *For all of God's promises have been fulfilled in Christ with a resounding "Yes!" And through Christ, our "Amen" (which means "Yes") ascends to God for his glory* (2 Cor. 1:20 NLT).

Page 65: *Now thanks be to God who always leads us in triumph in Christ* (2 Cor. 2:14 NKJV).

Page 143: *So we do not lose heart. Though our outer self is wasting away, our inner self is being renewed day by day* (2 Cor. 4:16 ESV).

Page 198: *For we walk by faith, not by sight* (2 Cor. 5:7 ESV).

Page 169: *For we walk by faith, not by sight* (2 Cor. 5:7 KJV).

Page 124: *Therefore, if anyone is in Christ, he is a new creation. The old has passed away; behold, the new has come* (2 Cor. 5:17 ESV).

Page 217: *This means that anyone who belongs to Christ has become a new person. The old life is gone; a new life has begun!* (2 Cor. 5:17 NLT).

Pages 58, 104: *We are therefore Christ's ambassadors, as though God were making his appeal through us. We implore you on Christ's behalf: Be reconciled to God* (2 Cor. 5:20).

Page 106: *You must each decide in your heart how much to give. And don't give reluctantly or in response to pressure. "For God loves a person who gives cheerfully"* (2 Cor. 9:7 NLT).

Page 107: *And God will generously provide all you need. Then you will always have everything you need and plenty left over to share with others* (2 Cor. 9:8 NLT).

Page 224: *Thanks be to God for his inexpressible gift!* (2 Cor. 9:15 ESV).

Page 163: *My grace is enough; it's all you need. My strength comes into its own in your weakness* (2 Cor. 12:9 MSG).

Page 200: *For when I am weak, then I am strong* (2 Cor. 12:10).

Page 67: *Examine yourselves to see whether you are in the faith; test yourselves. Do you not realize that Christ Jesus is in you—unless, of course, you fail the test?* (2 Cor. 13:5).

D

Page 85: *Do not be afraid of them; the LORD your God himself will fight for you* (Deut. 3:22).

Page 49: *But if from there you seek the LORD your God, you will find him if you seek him with all your heart and with all your soul* (Deut. 4:29).

Page 28: *Be strong and courageous. Do not be afraid or terrified because of them, for the LORD your God goes with you; he will never leave you nor forsake you* (Deut. 31:6 NIV).

Page 143: *Be strong and courageous. Do not fear or be in dread of them, for it is the LORD your God who goes with you. He will not leave you or forsake you* (Deut. 31:6 ESV).

E

Page 21: *There is a time for everything, and a season for every activity under the heavens* (Eccles. 3:1).

Page 149: *Better to be criticized by a wise person than to be praised by a fool* (Eccles. 7:5 NLT).

Page 73: *Dead flies make a perfumer's oil stink, so a little foolishness is weightier than wisdom and honor* (Eccles. 10:1 NASB).

Page 71: *Let us praise God for his glorious grace, for the free gift he gave us in his dear Son!* (Eph. 1:6 GNT).

Page 162: *For by grace you have been saved through faith. And this is not your own doing; it is the gift of God* (Eph. 2:8 ESV).

Page 17: *For we are God's masterpiece. He has created us anew in Christ Jesus, so we can do the good things he planned for us long ago* (Eph. 2:10 NLT).

Page 19: *I pray that out of his glorious riches he may strengthen you with power through his Spirit in your inner being* (Eph. 3:16).

Page 106: *Now unto him that is able to do exceeding abundantly above all that we ask or think, according to the power that worketh in us* (Eph. 3:20 KJV).

Page 175: *Now to him who is able to do immeasurably more than all we ask or imagine, according to his power that is at work within us* (Eph. 3:20).

Page 93: *Let no corrupting talk come out of your mouths, but only such as is good for building up* (Eph. 4:29 ESV).

Page 135: *Be kind to one another, tenderhearted, forgiving one another, as God in Christ forgave you* (Eph. 4:32 ESV).

Page 44: *Wake up, sleeper, rise from the dead, and Christ will shine on you* (Eph. 5:14).

Page 138: *Making the best use of the time, because the days are evil* (Eph. 5:16 ESV).

Page 204, 210: *Make the most of every opportunity* (Eph. 5:16 NLT).

Page 193: *Look carefully then how you walk, not as unwise but as wise, making the best use of the time* (Eph. 5:15–16 ESV).

Page 87: *And the* LORD *said unto him, What is that in thine hand?* (Exod. 4:2 KJV).

Page 10: *You should also choose some of the people to be judges and leaders* (Exod. 18:21 ERV).

G

Page 32: *I have been crucified with Christ. It is no longer I who live, but Christ who lives in me. And the life I now live in the flesh I live by faith in the Son of God, who loved me and gave himself for me* (Gal. 2:20 ESV).

Page 56: *For in Christ Jesus you are all sons of God, through faith* (Gal. 3:26 ESV).

Page 164: *So I say, walk by the Spirit, and you will not gratify the desires of the flesh* (Gal. 5:16).

Page 83: *But the fruit of the Spirit is love, joy, peace, forbearance, kindness, goodness, faithfulness, gentleness and self-control* (Gal. 5:22–23).

Page 189: *Carry each other's burdens, and in this way you will fulfill the law of Christ* (Gal. 6:2).

Page 15: *Let us not grow weary of doing good, for in due season we will reap, if we do not give up* (Gal. 6:9 ESV).

Page 165: *So let's not get tired of doing what is good. At just the right time we will reap a harvest of blessing if we don't give up* (Gal. 6:9 NLT).

Page 190: *Go to the land that I will show you* (Gen. 12:1 NLT).

Page 12: *God has made laughter for me; everyone who hears will laugh with me* (Gen. 21:6 ESV).

H

Page 174: *Let us throw off everything that hinders and the sin that so easily entangles* (Heb. 12:1).

Page 88: *Therefore, since we are surrounded by such a great cloud of witnesses, let us throw off everything that hinders and the sin that so easily entangles. And let us run with perseverance the race marked out for us, fixing our eyes on Jesus, the pioneer and perfecter of faith* (Heb. 12:1–2).

Page 6: *For the Lord disciplines those he loves, and he punishes each one he accepts as his child* (Heb. 12:6 NLT).

Page 37: *And please God by worshiping him with holy fear and awe* (Heb. 12:28 NLT).

Page 194: *Keep your lives free from the love of money and be content with what you have* (Heb. 13:5).

Page 127: *And don't forget to do good and to share with those in need. These are the sacrifices that please God* (Heb. 13:16 NLT).

Page 187: *Do not neglect to do good and to share what you have, for such sacrifices are pleasing to God* (Heb. 13:16 ESV).

I

Page 16, 113: *Then I heard the voice of the Lord saying, "Whom shall I send? And who will go for us?" And I said, "Here am I. Send me!* (Isa. 6:8).

Page 79: *You will keep in perfect peace those whose minds are steadfast, because they trust in you* (Isa. 26:3).

Page 130: *Here a little, and there a little* (Isa. 28:10 KJV).

Page 132: *And your ears shall hear a word behind you, saying, "This is the way, walk in it," when you turn to the right or when you turn to the left* (Isa. 30:21 ESV).

Page 55: *But those who hope in the LORD will renew their strength. They will soar on wings like eagles; they will run and not grow weary, they will walk and not be faint* (Isa. 40:31).

Page 215: *But they that wait upon the LORD shall renew their strength; they shall mount up with wings as eagles; they shall run, and not be weary; and they shall walk, and not faint* (Isa. 40:31 KJV).

Page 189: *But they who wait for the* LORD *shall renew their strength; they shall mount up with wings like eagles; they shall run and not be weary* (Isa. 40:31 ESV).

Page 115: *Don't be afraid, for I am with you. Don't be discouraged, for I am your God. I will strengthen you and help you. I will hold you up with my victorious right hand* (Isa. 41:10 NLT).

Page 18: *Forget the former things; do not dwell on the past. See, I am doing a new thing!* (Isa. 43:18–19).

Page 213: *For I am about to do something new. See, I have already begun! Do you not see it? I will make a pathway through the wilderness. I will create rivers in the dry wasteland* (Isa. 43:19 NLT).

Page 134: *The Sovereign* LORD *has given me his words of wisdom, so that I know how to comfort the weary. Morning by morning he wakens me and opens my understanding to his will* (Isa. 50:4 NLT).

Page 109: *So shall My word be that goes forth out of My mouth: it shall not return to Me void [without producing any effect, useless], but it shall accomplish that which I please and purpose, and it shall prosper in the thing for which I sent it* (Isa. 55:11 AMPC).

Page 137: *To give unto them beauty for ashes* (Isa. 61:3 KJV).

Page 51: *And you will be called priests of our* LORD, *you will be named ministers of our God* (Isa. 61:6).

J

Page 16: *Because you know that the testing of your faith produces perseverance* (James 1:3).

Page 195: *If you need wisdom, ask our generous God, and he will give it to you* (James 1:5 NLT).

Page 225: *Every good thing given and every perfect gift is from above, coming down from the Father of lights, with whom there is no variation or shifting shadow* (James 1:17 NASB).

Page 108: *Anyone who listens to the word but does not do what it says is like* someone who looks at his face in a mirror and, after looking at himself, goes away and immediately forgets what he looks like (James 1:23–24).

Page 22: *For if anyone is a hearer of the word and not a doer, he is like a man who looks intently at his natural face in a mirror. For he looks at himself and goes away and at once forgets what he was like* (James 1:23–24 ESV).

Page 31: *He was called a friend of God* (James 2:23 ESV).

Page 129, 191: *Draw near to God, and he will draw near to you. Cleanse your hands, you sinners, and purify your hearts, you double-minded* (James 4:8 ESV).

Page 139: *Humble yourselves before the Lord, and he will lift you up in honor* (James 4:10 NLT).

Page 11: *What is your life? You are a mist that appears for a little while and then vanishes* (James 4:14).

Page 119: *So whoever knows the right thing to do and fails to do it, for him it is sin* (James 4:17 ESV).

Page 186: *Remember, it is sin to know what you ought to do and then not do it* (James 4:17 NLT).

Page 24: *"For I know the plans I have for you," says the LORD. "They are plans for good and not for disaster, to give you a future and a hope"* (Jer. 29:11 NLT).

Page 72: *Ah, LORD God! It is you who have made the heavens and the earth by your great power and by your outstretched arm! Nothing is too hard for you* (Jer. 32:17 ESV).

Page 35: *Behold, I am the LORD, the God of all flesh. Is anything too hard for me?* (Jer. 32:27 ESV).

Page 167: *Call to me and I will answer you, and will tell you great and hidden things that you have not known* (Jer. 33:3 ESV).

Page 29: *If I say, "I will forget my complaint, I will put off my sad face, and be of good cheer"* (Job 9:27 ESV).

Page 222: *You may ask me for anything in my name, and I will do it* (John 14:14).

Page 76: *Let him not trust in emptiness, deceiving himself; For emptiness will be his reward* (Job 15:31 NASB).

Page 111: *The righteous keep moving forward* (Job 17:9 NLT).

Page 20: *Let me be weighed in an even balance that God may know mine integrity* (Job 31:6 KJV).

Page 60: *For the law was given by Moses, but grace and truth came by Jesus Christ* (John 1:17 KJV).

Page 72: *"Rabbi, you are the Son of God; you are the king of Israel." Jesus responded, "You believe because I told you I saw you under the fig tree. You will see greater things than that"* (John 1:49, 50).

Page 47: *He must increase, but I must decrease* (John 3:30 NKJV).

Page 202: *He must become greater and greater, and I must become less and less* (John 3:30 NLT).

Page 121: *He must become greater; I must become less* (John 3:30).

Page 47: *God is Spirit, and those who worship Him must worship in spirit and truth* (John 4:24 NKJV).

Page 91: *God is a Spirit: and they that worship him must worship him in spirit and in truth* (John 4:24 KJV).

Page 43: *Then Jesus explained, "My nourishment comes from doing the will of God, who sent me, and from finishing his work"* (John 4:34 NLT).

Page 214: *Your approval means nothing to me* (John 5:41 NLT).

Page 88: *Go now and leave your life of sin* (John 8:11).

Page 69: *I am the light of the world. If you follow me, you won't have to walk in darkness, because you will have the light that leads to life* (John 8:12 NLT).

Page 199: *And you will know the truth, and the truth will set you free* (John 8:32 ESV).

Page 192: *The thief comes only to steal and kill and destroy. I came that they may have life, and have it abundantly* (John 10:10 NRSV).

Page 120: *For they loved human praise more than praise from God* (John 12:43).

Page 62: *You can ask for anything in my name, and I will do it, so that the Son can bring glory to the Father* (John 14:13 NLT).

Page 225: *Whatever you ask in my name, this I will do, that the Father may be glorified in the Son* (John 14:13 ESV).

Page 116: *I am leaving you with a gift—peace of mind and heart. And the peace I give is a gift the world cannot give. So don't be troubled or afraid* (John 14:27 NLT).

Page 68: *When he [the Holy Spirit] comes, he will prove the world to be in the wrong about sin and righteousness and judgment* (John 16:8).

Page 13: *If we confess our sins, he is faithful and just and will forgive us our sins and purify us from all unrighteousness* (1 John 1:9).

Page 205: *All who have this hope in him purify themselves, just as he is pure* (1 John 3:3).

Page 141: *Let us not love with words or speech but with actions and in truth* (1 John 3:18).

Page 9: *Let us not love in word or talk but in deed and in truth* (1 John 3:18 ESV).

Page 173: *Let's not merely say that we love each other; let us show the truth by our actions* (1 John 3:18 NLT).

Page 134: *Whoever does not love does not know God, because God is love* (1 John 4:8).

Page 82: *This is the confidence we have in approaching God: that if we ask anything according to his will, he hears us. And if we know that he hears us—whatever we ask—we know that we have what we asked of him* (1 John 5:14–15).

Page 123: *And since we know he hears us when we make our requests, we also know that he will give us what we ask for* (1 John 5:15 NLT).

Page 179: *Be strong and courageous. Do not be afraid; do not be discouraged, for the LORD your God will be with you wherever you go* (Josh. 1:9).

Page 31: *On some have compassion, making a distinction; but others save with fear* (Jude 1:22–23 NKJV).

K

Page 1: *"I have had enough, L*ORD*," he said. "Take my life; I am no better than my ancestors"* (1 Kings 19:4).

L

Page 178, 225: *The L*ORD *is good to those who wait for him, to the soul who seeks him* (Lam. 3:25 ESV).

Page 158: *Blessed is he that shall eat bread in the kingdom of God* (Luke 14:15 ASV).

Page 27: *You must be holy because I, the L*ORD*, am holy. I have set you apart from all other people to be my very own* (Lev. 20:26 NLT).

Page 35, 46: *For nothing will be impossible with God* (Luke 1:37 ESV).

Page 60: *And as you wish that others would do to you, do so to them* (Luke 6:31 ESV).

Page 147: *Do to others as you would like them to do to you* (Luke 6:31 NLT).

Page 110: *Forgive, and you will be forgiven* (Luke 6:37).

Page 157: *Give, and it will be given to you. A good measure, pressed down, shaken together and running over, will be poured into your lap. For with the measure you use, it will be measured to you* (Luke 6:38).

Page 83: *No one lights a lamp and hides it in a clay jar or puts it under a bed. Instead, they put it on a stand, so that those who come in can see the light* (Luke 8:16).

Page 122: *So I say to you: Ask and it will be given to you; seek and you will find; knock and the door will be opened to you* (Luke 11:9).

Page 152: *Whoever is faithful in small matters will be faithful in large ones; whoever is dishonest in small matters will be dishonest in large ones* (Luke 16:10 GNT).

Page 184: *If you are faithful in little things, you will be faithful in large ones. But if you are dishonest in little things, you won't be honest with greater responsibilities* (Luke 16:10 NLT).

Page 140: *The apostles said to the Lord, "Increase our faith!"* (Luke 17:5 ESV).

Page 167: *For they have given a tiny part of their surplus, but she, poor as she is, has given everything she has* (Luke 21:4 NLT).

Page 185: *I have prayed for you, Simon [Peter] that your faith may not fail. And when you have turned back, strengthen your brothers* (Luke 22:32).

Page 153: *Please take this cup of suffering away from me. Yet I want your will to be done, not mine* (Luke 22:42 NLT).

M

Page 180: *I will pour out a blessing so great you won't have enough room to take it in! Try it! Put me to the test!* (Mal. 3:10 NLT).

Page 41: *"What sort of new teaching is this?" they asked excitedly. "It has such authority! Even evil spirits obey his orders!"* (Mark 1:27 NLT).

Page 22: Then He said to them, *"Take heed what you hear. With the same measure you use, it will be measured to you; and to you who hear, more will be given* (Mark 4:24 NKJV).

Page 89: *"A prophet is not without honor except in his own town"* (Mark 6:4).

Page 26: *Then Jesus said, "Let's go off by ourselves to a quiet place and rest awhile"* (Mark 6:31 NLT).

Page 38: *For what shall it profit a man, if he shall gain the whole world, and lose his own soul?* (Mark 8:36 KJV).

Page 64: *And Jesus said to him, "'If you can'! All things are possible for one who believes"* (Mark 9:23 ESV).

Page 89: *Everything is possible for one who believes* (Mark 9:23).

Page 113: *Peter began to say to Him, "Behold, we have left everything and followed You"* (Mark 10:28 NASB).

Page 62: *Therefore I tell you, whatever you ask for in prayer, believe that you have received it, and it will be yours* (Mark 11:24).

Page 14: *He [Jesus] said to them, "Go into all the world and preach the gospel to all creation* (Mark 16:15).

Page 196: *Go into all the world and preach the Good News to everyone* (Mark 16:15 NLT).

Page 66: *"Come, follow me," Jesus said, "and I will send you out to fish for people"* (Matt. 4:19).

Page 109: *Blessed are the poor [the humble] in spirit, for theirs is the kingdom of heaven* (Matt. 5:3 ESV).

Page 228: *Blessed are those who hunger and thirst for righteousness, for they shall be satisfied* (Matt. 5:6 ESV).

Page 57: *But let your statement be, "Yes, yes" or "No, no"; anything beyond these is of evil* (Matt. 5:37 NASB).

Page 88: *But I say, love your enemies! Pray for those who persecute you!* (Matt. 5:44 NLT).

Page 199: *But when you give to someone in need, don't let your left hand know what your right hand is doing* (Matt. 6:3 NLT).

Page 50: *Can any one of you by worrying add a single hour to your life?* (Matt. 6:27).

Page 19: *Seek first his kingdom and his righteousness, and all these things will be given to you* (Matt. 6:33).

Page 50: *Therefore do not worry about tomorrow, for tomorrow will worry about itself. Each day has enough trouble of its own* (Matt. 6:34).

Page 53: *Don't pick on people, jump on their failures, criticize their faults—unless, of course, you want the same treatment* (Matt. 7:1 MSG).

Page 46: *Keep on knocking, and the door will be opened to you* (Matt. 7:7 NLT).

Page 65: *If you, then, though you are evil, know how to give good gifts to your children, how much more will your Father in heaven give good gifts to those who ask him!* (Matt. 7:11).

Page 96: *By their fruit you will recognize them* (Matt. 7:16).

Page 56: *Whoever finds his life will lose it, and whoever loses his life for my sake will find it* (Matt. 10:39 ESV).

Page 19: *Whoever finds his [lower] life will lose it [the higher life], and whoever loses his [lower] life on My account will find it [the higher life]* (Matt. 10:39 AMPC).

Page 172: *Come to me, all you who are weary and burdened, and I will give you rest* (Matt. 11:28).

Page 207: *For my yoke is easy to bear, and the burden I give you is light* (Matt. 11:30 NLT).

Page 155: *Then Jesus said to his disciples, "If any of you wants to be my follower, you must give up your own way, take up your cross, and follow me"* (Matt. 16:24 NLT).

Page 129: *For where two or three are gathered in my name, there am I among them* (Matt. 18:20 ESV).

Page 176: *For where two or three have gathered together in My name, I am there in their midst* (Matt. 18:20 NASB).

Page 78: *With God all things are possible* (Matt. 19:26 NKJV).

Page 137: *I tell you the truth, if you have faith and don't doubt, you can do things like this and much more* (Matt. 21:21 NLT).

Pages 13, 25: *And whatever you ask in prayer, you will receive, if you have faith* (Matt. 21:22 ESV).

Page 131: *If you believe, you will receive whatever you ask for in prayer* (Matt. 21:22).

Pages 101, 166: *The master said, "Well done, my good and faithful servant. You have been faithful in handling this small amount, so now I will give you many more responsibilities. Let's celebrate together!"* (Matt. 25:23 NLT).

Page 123: *To those who use well what they are given, even more will be given, and they will have an abundance. But from those who do nothing, even what little they have will be taken away* (Matt. 25:29 NLT).

N

Page 73: *"Go and enjoy choice food and sweet drinks. . . . Do not grieve, for the joy of the LORD is your strength"* (Neh. 8:10).

Page 161: *For the joy of the LORD is your strength* (Neh. 8:10).

Page 181: *GOD bless you and keep you, GOD smile on you and gift you, GOD look you full in the face and make you prosper* (Num. 6:24–26 MSG).

P

Page 211: *These trials will show that your faith is genuine. It is being tested as fire tests and purifies gold—though your faith is far more precious than mere gold. So when your faith remains strong through many trials, it will bring you much praise and glory and honor on the day when Jesus Christ is revealed to the whole world* (1 Pet. 1:7 NLT).

Page 169: *For you were straying like sheep, but have now returned to the Shepherd and Overseer of your souls* (1 Pet. 2:25 ESV).

Page 71: *Do not repay evil with evil or insult with insult. On the contrary, repay evil with blessing, because to this you were called so that you may inherit a blessing* (1 Pet. 3:9).

Page 128: *Always be prepared to give an answer to everyone who asks you to give the reason for the hope that you have. But do this with gentleness and respect* (1 Pet. 3:15).

Page 55: *If anyone serves, they should do so with the strength God provides, so that in all things God may be praised through Jesus Christ* (1 Pet. 4:11).

Page 35: *Humble yourselves, therefore, under God's mighty hand, that He may lift you up in due time* (1 Pet. 5:6).

Page 24: *Be alert and of sober mind. Your enemy the devil prowls around like a roaring lion looking for someone to devour* (1 Pet. 5:8).

Page 97: *May you always be filled with the fruit of your salvation—the righteous character produced in your life by Jesus Christ—for this will bring much glory and praise to God* (Phil. 1:11 NLT).

Page 158: *Do nothing from selfish ambition or conceit, but in humility count others more significant than yourselves* (Phil. 2:3 ESV).

Page 220: *Let each of you look not only to his own interests, but also to the interests of others* (Phil. 2:4 ESV).

Page 186: *For God is working in you, giving you the desire and the power to do what pleases him* (Phil. 2:13 NLT).

Page 90: *Have this attitude in yourselves which was also in Christ Jesus* (Phil. 2:5 NASB).

Page 208: *Do everything without complaining* (Phil. 2:14 NLT).

Page 8: *But I focus on this one thing: Forgetting the past and looking forward to what lies ahead* (Phil. 3:13 NLT).

Page 219: *Forgetting what is behind and straining toward what is ahead* (Phil. 3:13).

Page 64: *I press on toward the goal for the prize of the upward call of God in Christ Jesus* (Phil. 3:14 ESV).

Page 73: *Rejoice in the Lord always. I will say it again: Rejoice!* (Phil. 4:4).

Page 141: *Don't worry about anything; instead, pray about everything. Tell God what you need, and thank him for all he has done* (Phil. 4:6 NLT).

Page 37: *Do not be anxious about anything, but in every situation, by prayer and petition, with thanksgiving, present your requests to God* (Phil. 4:6).

Page 165: *Do not be anxious about anything, but in everything by prayer and supplication with thanksgiving let your requests be made known to God. And the peace of God, which surpasses all understanding, will guard your hearts and your minds in Christ Jesus* (Phil. 4:6–7 ESV).

Page 201: *And the peace of God, which transcends all understanding, will guard your hearts and your minds in Christ Jesus* (Phil. 4:7).

Page 212: *And the peace of God, which surpasses all understanding, will guard your hearts and your minds in Christ Jesus* (Phil. 4:7 ESV).

Page 114: *Finally, brothers, whatever is true, whatever is noble, whatever is right, whatever is pure, whatever is lovely, whatever is admirable—if anything is excellent or praiseworthy—think about such things* (Phil. 4:8).

Page 210: *For I have learned how to be content with whatever I have* (Phil. 4:11 NLT).

Page 19, 177: *I can do all things through Christ who strengthens me* (Phil. 4:13 NKJV).

Page 66: *And my God will meet all your needs according to the riches of his glory in Christ Jesus* (Phil. 4:19).

Page 94: *Let the wise listen and add to their learning, and let the discerning get guidance* (Prov. 1:5).

Page 182: *Let the wise hear and increase in learning, and the one who understands obtain guidance* (Prov. 1:5 ESV).

Page 29: *Cry out for insight, and ask for understanding. Search for them as you would for silver; seek them like hidden treasures* (Prov. 2:3–4 NLT).

Page 133: *Search for them as you would for silver; seek them like hidden treasures* (Prov. 2:4 NLT).

Page 11: *Trust in the Lord with all your heart, and do not lean on your own understanding* (Prov. 3:5 ESV).

Page 132: *Trust in the Lord with all your heart; do not depend on your own understanding. Seek his will in all you do, and he will show you which path to take* (Prov. 3:5–6 NLT).

Page 108: *Do not withhold good from those who deserve it when it's in your power to help them* (Prov. 3:27 NLT).

Page 222: *Do not withhold good from those to whom it is due, when it is in your power to do it* (Prov. 3:27 ESV).

Page 86: *Keep thy heart with all diligence; for out of it are the issues of life* (Prov. 4:23 KJV).

Page 74: *Keep vigilant watch over your heart; that's where life starts* (Prov. 4:23 MSG).

Page 144: *The hopes of the godly result in happiness, but the expectations of the wicked come to nothing* (Prov. 10:28 NLT).

Page 179: *Whoever refreshes others will be refreshed* (Prov. 11:25).

Page 219: *The hand of the diligent will rule* (Prov. 12:24 ESV).

Page 50: *A wise man thinks ahead; a fool doesn't, and even brags about it!* (Prov. 13:16 TLB).

Page 102: *Walk with the wise and become wise, for a companion of fools suffers harm* (Prov. 13:20).

Page 111: *Walk with the wise and become wise; associate with fools and get in trouble* (Prov. 13:20 NLT).

Page 126: *Whoever walks with the wise becomes wise, but the companion of fools will suffer harm* (Prov. 13:20 ESV).

Page 150: *A peaceful heart leads to a healthy body; jealousy is like cancer in the bones* (Prov. 14:30 NLT).

Page 26: *The ear that listens to life-giving reproof will dwell among the wise* (Prov. 15:31 ESV).

Page 168: *Commit your actions to the LORD, and your plans will succeed* (Prov. 16:3 NLT).

Page 102, 170: *We can make our plans, but the LORD determines our steps* (Prov. 16:9 NLT).

Page 97: *Gracious words are like a honeycomb, sweetness to the soul and health to the body* (Prov. 16:24 ESV).

Page 48: *A brother is born to help in time of need* (Prov. 17:17 NLT).

Page 30: *There are "friends" who destroy each other, but a real friend sticks closer than a brother* (Prov. 18:24 NLT).

Page 183: *A man who has friends must himself be friendly* (Prov. 18:24 NKJV).

Page 209: *One who has unreliable friends soon comes to ruin, but there is a friend who sticks closer than a brother* (Prov. 18:24).

Page 86: *Whoever is kind to the poor lends to the LORD, and he will reward them for what they have done* (Prov. 19:17).

Page 188: *Listen to advice and accept instruction, that you may gain wisdom in the future* (Prov. 19:20 ESV).

Page 6: *Many are the plans in a person's heart, but it is the LORD's purpose that prevails* (Prov. 19:21).

Page 171: *Many are the plans in the mind of a man, but it is the purpose of the LORD that will stand* (Prov. 19:21 ESV).

Page 45: *Many plans are in a man's mind, but it is the Lord's purpose for him that will stand* (Prov. 19:21 AMPC).

Page 77: *The horse is prepared for the day of battle, but the victory belongs to the LORD* (Prov. 21:31 NLT).

Page 151: *For the righteous falls seven times and rises again* (Prov. 24:16 ESV).

Page 121: *It's not good to eat too much honey, and it's not good to seek honors for yourself* (Prov. 25:27 NLT).

Page 54: *Let another praise you, and not your own mouth; a stranger, and not your own lips* (Prov. 27:2 ESV).

Page 135: *Faithful are the wounds of a friend* (Prov. 27:6 KJV).

Page 68: *Wait for the LORD; Be strong and let your heart take courage; Yes, wait for the LORD* (Ps. 27:14 NASB).

Page 159: *As iron sharpens iron, so one person sharpens another* (Prov. 27:17).

Page 36: *Where there is no prophetic vision the people cast off restraint, but blessed is he who keeps the law* (Prov. 29:18 ESV).

Pages 52, 198: *Where there is no vision, the people perish* (Prov. 29:18 KJV).

Page 212: *But you, O LORD, are a shield about me, my glory, and the lifter of my head* (Ps. 3:3 ESV).

Page 23: *For You, Lord, will bless the [uncompromisingly] righteous [him who is upright and in right standing with You]; as with a shield You will surround him with goodwill (pleasure and favor)* (Ps. 5:12 AMPC).

Page 15: *I will praise you, LORD, with all my heart; I will tell of all the marvelous things you have done* (Ps. 9:1 NLT).

Page 172: *The LORD is a stronghold for the oppressed, a stronghold in times of trouble* (Ps. 9:9 ESV).

Page 39: *The heavens proclaim the glory of God. The skies display his craftsmanship* (Ps. 19:1 NLT).

Page 94: *Turn to me and be gracious to me, for I am lonely and afflicted* (Ps. 25:16).

Page 142: *What, what would have become of me] had I not believed that I would see the Lord's goodness in the land of the living!* (Ps. 27:13 AMPC).

Page 21: *Weeping may stay for the night, but rejoicing comes in the morning* (Ps. 30:5).

Page 9: *The LORD says, "I will guide you along the best pathway for your life. I will advise you and watch over you"* (Ps. 32:8 NLT).

Page 145: *I will instruct you and teach you in the way you should go; I will counsel you with my loving eye on you* (Ps. 32:8).

Page 185: *Come, let us tell of the LORD's greatness; let us exalt his name together* (Ps. 34:3 NLT).

Page 149: *Take delight in the LORD, and He will give you your heart's desires* (Ps. 37:4 NLT).

Page 109: *Be still before the LORD and wait patiently for him* (Ps. 37:7 ESV).

Page 87: *The LORD makes firm the steps of the one who delights in him* (Ps. 37:23).

Page 140: *The LORD directs the steps of the godly. He delights in every detail of their lives* (Ps. 37:23 NLT).

Page 79: *The LORD makes firm the steps of the one who delights in him; though he may stumble, he will not fall, for the Lord upholds him with his hand* (Ps. 37:23–24).

Page 51: *And now, Lord, what do I wait for and expect? My hope and expectation are in you* (Ps. 39:7 AMPC).

Page 5: *As the deer pants for streams of water, so my soul pants for you, my God* (Ps. 42:1).

Page 136: *For the LORD Most High is awesome* (Ps. 47:2 NLT).

Page148: *Create in me a clean heart, O God. Renew a loyal spirit within me* (Ps. 51:10 NLT).

Page 20: *Restore to me the joy of your salvation, and uphold me with a willing spirit* (Ps. 51:12 ESV).

Page 61: *Give your burdens to the LORD, and he will take care of you. He will not permit the godly to slip and fall* (Ps. 55:22 NLT).

Page 100: *When I am afraid, I will put my trust in You* (Ps. 56:3 NASB).

Page 155: *When I am afraid, I put my trust in you* (Ps. 56:3).

Page 192: *Let all that I am wait quietly before God, for my hope is in him* (Ps. 62:5 NLT).

Page 69: *For the LORD God is a sun and shield; the LORD bestows favor and honor. No good thing does he withhold from those who walk uprightly* (Ps. 84:11 ESV).

Page 63: *For the LORD God is a sun and shield; the LORD bestows favor and honor; no good thing does he withhold from those whose walk is blameless* (Ps. 84:11).

Page 91: *So teach us to number our days that we may get a heart of wisdom* (Ps. 90:12 ESV).

Page 5: *Satisfy us in the morning with your steadfast love, that we may rejoice and be glad all our days* (Ps. 90:14 ESV).

Page 156: *When anxiety was great within me, your consolation brought me joy* (Ps. 94:19).

Page 80: *This is the day that the LORD has made; let us rejoice and be glad in it* (Ps. 118:24 ESV).

Page 205: *This is the day which the LORD has made; let us rejoice and be glad in it* (Ps. 118:24 NASB).

Page 92: *Your word is a lamp for my feet, a light on my path* (Ps. 119:105).

Page 8: *Lift up your hands toward the sanctuary, and praise the LORD* (Ps. 134:2 NLT).

Page 34: *I praise you, for I am fearfully and wonderfully made* (Ps. 139:14 ESV).

Page 67: *Thank you for making me so wonderfully complex! Your workmanship is marvelous—how well I know it* (Ps. 139:14 NLT).

Page 67: *I praise you because I am fearfully and wonderfully made; your works are wonderful, I know that full well* (Ps. 139:14).

Page 56: *Search me, God, and know my heart; test me and know my anxious thoughts. See if there is any offensive way in me, and lead me in the way everlasting* (Ps. 139:23–24).

Page 113: *Teach me to do your will, for you are my God! Let your good Spirit lead me on level ground!* (Ps. 143:10 ESV).

Page 74: *I will extol you, my God and King, and bless your name forever and ever* (Ps. 145:1 ESV).

Page 146: *The Lord is good to all, and His tender mercies are over all His works [the entirety of things created]* (Ps. 145:9 AMPC).

Page 202: *The LORD helps the fallen and lifts those bent beneath their loads* (Ps. 145:14 NLT).

Page 180: *The LORD is near to all who call on him* (Ps. 145:18 ESV).

Page 57: *He heals the brokenhearted and binds up their wounds* (Ps. 147:3 ESV).

R

Page 214: *I have placed before you an open door that no one can shut* (Rev. 3:8).

Page 228: *I have set before you an open door, which no one is able to shut* (Rev. 3:8 ESV).

Page 18: *I am the Alpha and the Omega, the First and the Last, the Beginning and the End* (Rev. 22:13).

Page 41: *For I am not ashamed of the gospel, because it is the power of God that brings salvation to everyone who believes* (Rom. 1:16).

Page 93: *Not only that, but we rejoice in our sufferings, knowing that suffering produces endurance, and endurance produces character, and character produces hope* (Rom. 5:3–4 ESV).

Page 49: *There is therefore now no condemnation to them which are in Christ Jesus, who walk not after the flesh, but after the Spirit* (Rom. 8:1 KJV).

Page 105: *Therefore, [there is] now no condemnation (no adjudging guilty of wrong) for those who are in Christ Jesus, who live [and] walk not after the dictates of the flesh, but after the dictates of the Spirit* (Rom. 8:1 AMPC).

Page 63: *But if Christ is in you, then even though your body is subject to death because of sin, the spirit gives life because of righteousness* (Rom. 8:10).

Page 136: *For I consider that the sufferings of this present time are not worth comparing with the glory that is to be revealed to us* (Rom. 8:18 ESV).

Page 178: *Yet what we suffer now is nothing compared to the glory he will reveal to us later* (Rom. 8:18 NLT).

Page 99, 203: *And we know that God causes everything to work together for the good of those who love God and are called according to his purpose for them* (Rom. 8:28 NLT).

Page 125: *And we know that in all things God works for the good of those who love him, who have been called according to his purpose* (Rom. 8:28).

Page 171: *If God is for us, who can ever be against us?* (Rom. 8:31 NLT).

Page 179: *Overwhelming victory is ours through Christ, who loved us* (Rom. 8:37 NLT).

Page 75: *So faith comes from hearing, and hearing through the word of Christ* (Rom. 10:17 ESV).

Page 81: *Therefore, I urge you, brothers and sisters, in view of God's mercy, to offer your bodies as a living sacrifice, holy and pleasing to God—this is your true and proper worship* (Rom. 12:1).

Page 83: *Do not conform to the pattern of this world, but be transformed by the renewing of your mind. Then you will be able to test and approve what God's will is—his good, pleasing and perfect will* (Rom. 12:2).

Page 147: *Do not be conformed to this world* (Rom. 12:2 ESV).

Page 151: *Let God transform you into a new person by changing the way you think. Then you will learn to know God's will for you, which is good and pleasing and perfect* (Rom. 12:2 NLT).

Page 120: *Rejoice in hope, be patient in tribulation, be constant in prayer* (Rom. 12:12 ESV).

Page 206: *Be happy with those who are happy, and weep with those who weep* (Rom. 12:15 NLT).

Page 146: *Don't let evil conquer you, but conquer evil by doing good* (Rom. 12:21 NLT).

Page 192: *Do not be overcome by evil, but overcome evil with good* (Rom. 12:21 ESV).

Page 43: *Do not be overcome by evil, but overcome evil with good* (Rom. 12:21 NKJV).

Page 53: *May the God of endurance and encouragement grant you to live in such harmony with one another, in accord with Christ Jesus, that together you may with one voice glorify the God and Father of our Lord Jesus Christ* (Rom. 15:5–6 ESV).

S

Page 67: *You know what your servant is really like, Sovereign LORD* (2 Sam. 7:20 NLT).

T

Page 153: *Therefore encourage one another and build each other up, just as in fact you are doing* (1 Thess. 5:11).

Page 187: *So encourage each other and build each other up* (1 Thess. 5:11 NLT).

Page 218: *Rejoice always, pray without ceasing, give thanks in all circumstances; for this is the will of God in Christ Jesus for you* (1 Thess. 5:16–18 ESV).

Page 217: *Pray without ceasing* (1 Thess. 5:17 ESV).

Page 84: *So then, brothers and sisters, stand firm and hold fast to the teachings we passed on to you, whether by word of mouth or by letter* (2 Thess. 2:15).

Page 168: *Do not grow weary in doing good* (2 Thess. 3:13 ESV).

Page 127: *Command them to do good, to be rich in good deeds, and to be generous and willing to share* (1 Tim. 6:18).

Page 22: *But continue thou in the things which thou hast learned and hast been assured of, knowing of whom thou hast learned them* (2 Tim. 3:14 KJV).

Page 61: *In everything set them an example by doing what is good. In your teaching show integrity, seriousness and soundness of speech that cannot be condemned, so that those who oppose you may be ashamed because they have nothing bad to say about us* (Titus 2:7–8).

Page 119: *Our people must learn to do good by meeting the urgent needs of others; then they will not be unproductive* (Titus 3:14 NLT).

Z

Page 208: *The LORD your God in your midst, The Mighty One, will save* (Zeph. 3:17 NKJV).

SUBJECT INDEX

Relying on trusted friends: December 1
Removing weights: October 8
Repentance: March 15, September 19
Repenting: September 9
Rest: February 4
Resting: November 3, December 17
Rivalries: December 18

S

Sacrifice: September 26
Salvation: January 15
Sanctification: May 6, November 27
Satan: February 1
Satisfaction: January 1
Seeing God as your friend: December 27
Seeing ourselves with God's eyes: June 23
Seeing with God's eyes: March 20, August 18, December 12
Seeking God: March 16
Self-confidence: December 8, December 12
Self-control: February 23, August 25
Self-sufficency: February 23
Self-worth: June 23, October 10
Serving God: March 19
Serving God in faith: September 26
Serving others: July 25, September 11, October 15, October 17
Setting our sights on Heaven: December 28
Shedding weights: September 8
Sin: January 30, May 21, June 18, July 28, August 14, September 9,
    September 19, October 1, November 21, December 22, December 30
Sleepwalking: March 6
Small actions that make a difference: October 23
Sold out for God: April 19, June 8, June 22
Spiritual battles: May 13, May 15, May 21
Spiritual gifts: October 26, December 23
Spiritual growth: January 18, February 3, March 28, April 29, May 7,
    May 10, May 13, June 9, August 20, September 21, October 31,
    November 27

CPSIA information can be obtained
at www.ICGtesting.com
Printed in the USA
BVHW051417040821
613439BV00007B/720